To Mary Ann, Vince and Jason
and
To Heather and Laurel

Thank you for your inspiration
and
performance support

TURNING
RESEARCH
INTO *RESULTS*

A Guide
to Selecting
the Right
Performance
Solutions

TURNING
RESEARCH
INTO RESULTS

A Guide
to Selecting
the Right
Performance
Solutions

Richard E. Clark and Fred Estes

INFORMATION AGE PUBLISHING, INC.
Charlotte, NC • www.infoagepub.com

ISBN: 978-1-59311-991-1

Printed in the United States of America

Contents

Acknowledgments

We want to acknowledge our debt to a number of individuals and groups who helped us develop and elaborate many of the ideas in this book.

Our first obligation is to the extraordinary professionals who became students in the human performance doctoral program in the Rossier School of Education at the University of Southern California over the past 15 years. Their willingness to engage in a dialogue with us about performance at work has been vital to the development of our thinking. Something very special happens when a diverse group of established and skilled professionals come back to a good university to get an advanced degree. More new knowledge is generated than is "taught." Dr. Dan Blair, one of our friends in this group, was responsible for connecting us with our publisher Seth Leibler and his superb staff of editors, marketing people, and designers at CEP Press. Suzanne Bennett and Jill Russell of CEP Press made substantive contributions to the organization and clarity of what we wrote. We might not have written the book without Dan's initiative and encouragement.

We also feel beholden to our colleagues who conduct and publish research on human performance. One of our primary goals is to create a much wider and more appreciative audience for that research. We believe that it is difficult for rational people to discount the value of research-based knowledge once the evidence for its impact is presented. We only hope we have the skill to describe your work accurately and persuasively.

Finally and most important, we want to acknowledge what we've learned from our clients. Information gained from research has to be translated, implemented, and studied in real organizations struggling with tangible performance issues. Our collaboration with professional colleagues working in interesting organizations has allowed us to put shape and substance to many of our strategies. Some of you may notice one or two shared experiences from your organization are "sanitized" and described in the case studies at the end of the book. Thank you for the opportunity to work with and learn from you.

Richard E. Clark
Fred Estes

Introduction and Overview
2009 Edition

THE GOAL OF THIS BOOK is to describe how you can adopt the results of solid performance research and turn it into practical, and cost-beneficial performance results for your organization.

A review of this book by Dr. Brenda Sugrue (currently Director of Instructional Systems for Ford Motor Company—formerly a training manager for IBM and a professor at the University of Iowa) described it in the following way:

> This book is all you need to understand the process of performance improvement in organizations, and the "active ingredients" that impact performance. The book separates the snake oil and fads from solutions that are supported by research. It gives clear and research-based guidelines for diagnosing the causes of performance gaps and selecting solutions for knowledge, motivation, and organizational problems. Case studies illustrate the application of the model and rules. In addition, the book describes how to reliably and validly evaluate the effects of performance solutions and identifies flaws in some common approaches to evaluation. The book answers the kinds of "why" and "what if" questions that rarely get addressed. It includes a powerful model of motivated performance that can be used to address any motivational problems. (It provides the reader with) the arguments and references to support organizational development and training practices and also the arguments and evidence to abandon practices that have been shown to either be ineffective or to do more harm than good. If you want to understand why what you are doing works (or doesn't work), you need to read this book. It is unlike any other to date in the field of performance improvement and training. It takes the profession to a higher level and is a must for anyone working in the area of organizational development, performance improvement, or training.

While the examples and case studies in the book come from business settings, we've heard from readers who have used our gap-analysis approach successfully in education (K–12 and Higher Education) and Government (military as well as federal, state and local government offices). We have been surprised at the number of people who have told us that they use the approach at home and in their volunteer work.

Why Read This Book?

Research evidence dramatically increases the chance that a performance improvement program will succeed. The result of well-designed research provides guidance for decades—until new paradigms are developed and tested—just as Newtonian physics has worked for a very long time even though Einstein's work on relativity is needed to explain phenomena at a higher level.

We describe evidence and examples from the best research on how our knowledge and our motivation operate in different types of organizations to promote (or discourage) maximum performance. We identify performance improvement opportunities and problems and give clear advice about how to select tested strategies, products and services that will achieve performance levels required to support your organizational goals. We provide clear examples from areas such as sales, customer service and manufacturing about how to use the approach they suggest. At the end of most chapters you will find suggested resources for additional reading and research. This brief introduction provides a description of chapter content and the reason for the book.

Chapter Content

The book begins by presenting evidence that research-based and tested performance improvement strategies will work and are cost effective. The early chapters are based on a tested process for analyzing and achieving organizational goals. The authors make the point that increased performance at work requires clear "up front" goals for the organization and for every division, team and individual working in organizations. Once goals are available and the gap between goals and current performance is measured, they demonstrate how to analyze the amount and type of knowledge, motivation and organizational change necessary to reach the level of performance that will achieve those goals.

Chapter One lays the groundwork with evidence that research-based products have a significantly greater chance than any other approach of effectively increasing performance and adding to your bottom line.

Chapter Two begins with a review of a strategy for setting organizational and human performance goals and describes ways to determine both the cost-benefit and the impact of different types of goals on performance.

Chapter Three presents an approach to analyzing the performance goals you set by contrasting future plans with current levels of achievement—a technique often called "gap analysis." The objective of this exercise is to get a fix on the distance between current performance and the level required to achieve goals. Also, Chapter Three describes ways to determine the cause of gaps between desired performance goals and current performance levels. The argument is made that three critical ingredients influence all work performance—our knowledge, our motivation and the organizational environment where we work.

Chapter Four presents the results of research on the impact of different types of knowledge on performance in order to determine how and when to use training to achieve performance goals. This chapter describes some new ideas about the learning of complex knowledge, factors that promote the effective use of experts and leverage their advanced expertise, and why training sometimes fails in organizations. Sadly, many of the performance interventions in use today are based on obsolete and inadequate models of knowledge or motivation.

Chapter Five summarizes current research on work motivation and its impact on achievement. Exciting new insights are presented about established techniques such as incentive programs, employee empowerment strategies and the importance of worker confidence and trust.

Chapter Six summarizes advice from well-designed organizational change and development studies. Chapter Seven brings the discussion full circle with a system for evaluating performance and assessing its contribution to the achievement of organizational goals. In business organizations these goals are most often focused on income, market share and shareholder or investor value—areas where performance interventions have often failed to show an effect.

In the last part of the book, three chapters present case studies that illustrate both the gap analysis process, the selection of research-tested performance improvement "ingredients" in products and services for three different types or divisions of businesses. Chapter Eight describes the application of the ideas in the book to a manufacturing setting. Chapter Nine presents a case study describing a customer service issue. Chapter Ten applies the approach to a problem in a sales organization. Finally, Chapter Eleven is an attempt to capture and summarize the essence of the approach we are recommending.

This book presents solid, current research that forms the basis for ways to "engineer" maximum performance and ways to select products that reflect the best research and evaluation.

What is Unique About This Book?

Performance research provides a great deal of evidence that a significant number of very popular education and performance improvement products simply do not work. Chapter One describes a number of those failed approaches as part of the argument for the approach being recommended. Given the very rapid pace in most organizations today, change programs are quickly chosen and speedily applied. After what is often a great deal of effort and money spent, managers may feel there is no time to evaluate the results, especially if the primary customers fill in a questionnaire saying they are happy with the results. Yet there is research evidence (Clark, 1982) that reaction questionnaires (frequently called "smile sheets") often indicate the reverse of what actually happened. This means that programs that appear to have positive results can actually have caused significant problems or made the problem worse (changed by making this important point its own sentence and dropping parenthesis). It is painful to find that a very expensive program had no real impact so many vendors and customers are reluctant to go beyond the inadequate and often inaccurate "smile sheet" evaluation of performance improvement attempts. If the smile sheet result comes from a high profile organization, vendors use this information to continue to sell a performance product until the next fad emerges.

Sometimes performance products seem to get results in the same way that people occasionally recover from an illness if they are only given sugar pills—the so-called "placebo effect." Some performance interventions may appear to work if the results are not carefully evaluated by comparing them with viable alternatives. Why evaluate if the problem seems to be solved—who cares if a positive result came from an intervention that only served as a placebo? Is it possible that the product that appeared to solve a "self correcting" problem required unnecessary expense and afterwards is touted as successful and so becomes even more attractive to the next gullible adopter? There are many tested and powerful performance enhancement strategies that do work, so the book highlights these strategies and makes suggestions about how to select and apply tested strategies and products in practical situations.

National Academy of Sciences Review of Performance Research

The advice offered in this book is supported by evidence from a series of comprehensive reviews of available performance research. Many of these reviews are published in an excellent series of books offered by the U.S. National Academy of Sciences (NAS) and the National Research Council (NRC) and published through their National Academy Press in the 1990s. The NAS-NRC membership includes the top scientists in all fields drawn primarily from North America but also from many other countries. One of the goals of the Academy is to identify the best international research in many areas and translate it accurately for use in solving practical problems. To this end, the NRC appointed a committee of top researchers to review all studies in the areas of knowledge, motivation and organizational change, among other areas. The book draws heavily on these reviews. The background evidence for much of the advice you will find in the book is cited in each chapter so that if you wish, you can read the same material. The book also draws on a series of research reviews that are published in the best journals on performance issues in applied and experimental psychology, social and organizational psychology, sociology, performance improvement, training and development, business and related areas. These journals publish international research of the highest quality which is subjected to rigorous review by leading experts and is considered the best statement of what scientists know about a topic.

We also recommend that readers interested in the research background for our recommendations read an excellent recent book by two Stanford University Professors: *Hard Facts, Dangerous Half-Truths and Total Nonsense: Profiting from Evidence Based Management* (2006, Harvard Business School Press).

Giving the "Benefit of a Doubt" to Research Evidence

Misconceptions about exactly what happened during a performance improvement effort and why it happened are very common. It is possible for honest and intelligent people to misperceive results as they develop performance improvement programs. In fact, scientific methods were developed precisely because it is so easy and natural to misunderstand causes and misinterpret results. Aristotle, one of the greatest thinkers and problem solvers of all time, believed that a heavy object would fall faster than a lighter object. This assumption seemed logical to him and to nearly everyone at that time until actual research provided a different insight. Since Aristotle was so insightful and highly respected, all educated people took his word for it. Everyone, that is, until Galileo started testing this idea by actually dropping heavy and light objects and comparing their rate of fall. This empirical testing proved definitively that Aristotle was wrong.

The book constantly recommends that you demand proof. Either perform your own valid tests of performance interventions or leverage the work of those who have. Then evaluate all important and/or expensive performance improvement programs to insure that they work for you. One good test is worth a hundred opinions.

Best Practice—organizations who have tried some parts of this approach: In addition to research, the book also attempts to consider "best practice" and look at the impact of these ideas in real organizations. Human Resources managers and Training and Development managers often exchange ideas and report on what is working for their organization in professional journals and at professional conferences. Workshops and consulting on science-based, human performance improvement strategies are offered by two of the large professional organizations that support professionals in this area. Recent conferences and journal articles indicate that groups within the following organizations are adopting some of the recommended HPT strategies. In addition, books and articles often report the results of specific performance projects that are science-based. A short list of selected companies using HPT or a similar approach includes:

- IBM Global Services
- U.S. Marine Corps/1st Division
- U.S. Army, Training and Doctrine Command
- Sun Microsystems
- Santa Theresa High School/San Jose East Side Union School District
- Western Digital
- U.S. Navy Personnel Research and Development Center
- Amdahl Corporation
- Xerox Corporation
- Mercy Hospital, Iowa City
- University of Iowa
- J.D. Edwards (global software company)
- Toyota Motor Credit Corporation
- Hewlett-Packard Company
- Duke Power Company
- Eli Lilly & Company
- Banc One Corporation
- Trane Company (air-conditioning, heating & ventilating systems)
- Ernst & Young, LLP
- Sandia National Laboratory
- Mayo Clinics
- Microsoft Corporation
- Nortel Networks
- General Electric
- E*Trade
- SBC (parent of Southwestern Bell)
- Daimler Chrysler
- Blue Circle Canada (heavy building materials)
- USAID projects
- Steelcase (office furniture)
- Jack in the Box (fast food)
- Lockheed Martin
- Imperial Oil (Esso)

This list is by no means exhaustive, but does show the range of companies that have publicly presented the benefits of HPT to their company. This list includes high technology companies, dot coms, traditional manufacturers, financial companies, telecommunications, construction materials, fast foods, retailers, health care, consultancies, public sector organizations, international companies, and not-for-profits. Though HPT is applicable to companies large and small, the tools and methods in use at smaller companies are not so widely reported in journals and at conferences.

Knowing What We Know and What We Don't Know: Our Reason for Writing This Book

In the 1960s, when engineers around the world collaborated to send people to the moon and bring them back safely, everyone involved accepted the challenge with no clear idea of how they would accomplish the task. One plan was to modify an airplane for the moon mission. The largest aircraft at that time, the Boeing 707, however, had reached its limit of speed, payload and range; simply adding a bigger engine to the existing architecture would not work—a new paradigm was required. What was known about flight and about human performance at that point was not adequate for the challenge.

The success of the "mission to the moon" project in the 1960s was due, in large measure, to a system of classifying relevant knowledge into three categories:

1. What is "known to be known" (the well developed scientific knowledge base that is generally accepted);
2. What is "known to be unknown" (the current important questions that must be answered). These questions are critical even if the initial results of asking them are depressing; and finally,
3. What is "unknown to be unknown."

Our goal in this book is to draw on "what is known" through research and solid evaluation studies. The "what is known" in this area is so great that only the most important research findings are presented here. This research lays the foundation on which to build a solid framework for improving performance and organizational effectiveness. It forms the basis for our recommendations. The reference section provides the sources for those wishing to dig deeper into this the research.

A secondary aim of the book is to describe, "what is known to be unknown" about ways to enhance people's work performance. The "known to be unknown" marks the frontier of knowledge—a land of both danger and opportunity. There is danger because of the risks of the unknown. Our knowledge in this area is incomplete or inadequately tested. There is opportunity here to learn more and contribute to knowledge. As in the Old West of the American frontier, where the pioneers precede the map makers and the engineers, practitioners in organizations must work daily with problems where the state of knowledge is incomplete. We attempt to post signs at these performance improvement frontiers.

Finally, unknown mysteries cannot be discovered until researchers and practitioners clear up the "known to be unknown" questions. Often what is "unknown to be unknown" is first encountered when practitioners attempt to solve real world problems in real time.

For example, let's apply this same classification scheme with an earlier voyage of discovery, Columbus's voyage to discover a western route to the India and China. The technology of sailing ships was "known to be known" and judged adequate in terms of range and capacity. What lay far from shore in the Atlantic Ocean basin, however, was "known to be unknown" in central Europe. Would sailing ships fall off the edge of a flat earth? Would explorers encounter ship-destroying monsters or huge whirlpools? No one at that time and place knew. What no one suspected—what was "unknown to be unknown," at least in central Europe—was the existence of the North American continent. One result of the first of Columbus's voyages was to provide evidence that there was no edge and no monsters; the "known to be unknown" became "known to be known." From a central European perspective, the new continent moved into the "known to be unknown" category. You will find many examples of this phenomenon in performance improvement, illustrating one important way that practitioners and researchers collaborate in solving problems and in adding to our store of knowledge.

The book provides topics and questions that have special relevance to the problems and opportunities faced currently by trainers and performance improvement specialists in organizations that experience the greatest performance challenges. The book describes a number of general strategies that have achieved positive results in a majority of the solid research studies conducted in the field, in the laboratory and in real organizations.

This book emphasizes the "known to be known" information that might help you choose performance improvement products and services. Much of the information presented is well known to researchers but is almost unknown outside of research circles. Historians point out that information from research requires about one generation- about 20 years—to find its way into practice. This has been the case with everything from diet and smoking to the studies of mathematics and information sciences that lie at the root of modern computer systems. It is the goal of this book to speed up this cycle.

The book also attempts to identify the "known to be unknown" areas and suggest alternatives when research evidence is not yet available. Research exists to guide nearly all decisions about performance improvement, yet existing research is seldom conclusive. Thus the book attempts to describe the course of action that makes the most sense when our knowledge about what will solve a problem is incomplete.

Richard Clark and Fred Estes

1

Improving Performance: The Active Ingredients

THERE ARE HUGE NUMBERS of performance improvement products currently available in the performance marketplace. Many, but not most, of them will provide you with the performance improvement ingredients you need to achieve organizational goals. The trick is finding those that deliver. The purpose of this book is to help organizations make effective decisions about performance products and services. Rather than advocating one specific product or service, our strategy is to describe the "active ingredients" of effective products and processes—and let you match and locate those effective features in the services and products available.

While many products and services provide effective performance improvement strategies and features, all too many of them do not. Slick packaging and glitzy marketing can conceal fanciful or trendy notions that sound good but simply do not work. Some actually make performance worse, as we'll discuss later. This

1

book also helps you avoid the snake oil, the hucksters, and the honest vendors who unintentionally sell products that do not work. At the end of each chapter, we have also suggested some resources for further reading and to help you locate research that interests you.

Why Focus on Improved Performance?

Most business processes have their origins in the old idea that it is possible to automate the performance of employees. This thinking became popular in the early "assembly line" portion of the last century when most workers were not formally educated and had little organizational experience. Manufacturing required cooperation between many different jobs in order to produce a final product such as a car, and new training systems helped to regulate and standardize worker performance in order to produce reliable products. The capacity to ensure that everyone in a given job category performed the same job in the same way helped reduce the demand for educated workers. A guaranteed rate of pay (or piece work pay based on output) was adequate to motivate performance.

Many otherwise good managers today still believe that one only needs to train, pay people, and they should work effectively. Training and pay are viewed strictly as the costs of doing business and categorized as an expense. This results in the perception of employees as expensive necessities, not business resources that can increase income. The income side of business is presumed to result from products, not employees. This common model of the place of employees in a business is both outdated and dangerous.

Increasing knowledge, skills, and motivation—and focusing those assets on organizational goals—are the keys to success in the new world economy. During the next few decades, business will continue to focus on global competition, E-business, supply chain management, and strategic partnerships. Organizations will continue to face profound, complex, and persistent change. Nearly every sage and scientific study warns us that to achieve a sustainable competitive advantage in this permanent white-water environment, businesses must invest more and more resources in our knowledge workers. Knowledge workers are defined, in part, by the ability to solve new problems and adapt to changing conditions. In a constantly shifting economic marketplace, the most valuable workers are those who can change with it. We must improve the recruitment, management, development, motivation, support, and retention of the people who make a business successful.

The problem with this advice, in part, is that seasoned, productive people will always command premium compensation packages and have many options for great jobs. As the reward for solving complex problems and managing change effectively, knowledge workers want more autonomy and a piece of the action. Many of them realize that maximizing their contributions can be the critical edge successful businesses need. The demand for such workers creates a "War for Talent," as McKinsey & Company referred to it in a study of recruiting practices for knowledge workers (Chambers et al. 1998). In a recent follow-up study of recruiting practices for the best people, McKinsey found a discrepancy of 40 to 67 percent in the productivity of average versus high performers (Axelrod et al. 2001). No organization can afford downtime and lost productivity when introducing new products, implementing new strategies, or creating new businesses. You need your people to perform at their peak level all the time.

One way to determine whether greater attention to performance will protect and increase income is to ask one question: Can you standardize the behavior of employees through training and quality control measures to the extent that they will not have to solve novel problems or adapt to significant changes? If you *cannot* do that, it is absolutely necessary to think of employees as capital. Viewing employees as capital means looking at investments in performance improvement products as opportunities to produce income beyond the investment cost in the product. Investing in employees brings positive and profitable results for the organization. The new reality is that, in

ONE-THIRD OF PERFORMANCE FEEDBACK STRATEGIES MAKE PERFORMANCE WORSE.

Kluger and DiNisi's 1998 international review of well-designed performance feedback research studies produced a surprising insight. Performance feedback actually depressed performance in one-third of all feedback research studies conducted both in natural settings and in the laboratory. In another third of the studies, performance feedback had no impact. In only one-third of the studies did feedback increase performance. The problem appears to be caused by feedback that is not focused on clear performance goals and current performance results. In order to increase performance, performance feedback must be focused on closing the gap between goals and current progress. When feedback emphasizes the performer by pointing out poor performance or a lack of performance, or when it suggests that the performer is being held responsible for goals that were not clear initially, performance deteriorates. Kluger and DiNisi also emphasize that when employees felt their work performance was connected to their personal growth, performance feedback was most beneficial. The finding that poor feedback was obvious in two-thirds of all well-planned research studies suggests that it may even be more prevalent in practice, since researchers tend to select the best strategies to test in experiments.

Reference: Kluger, Avraham, and Angelo DiNisi. 1998. Feedback interventions: Toward the understanding of a double-edged sword. *Current Directions in Psychological Science* 7, no. 3: 67-72.

our knowledge-based economy, improving human performance is the highest leverage activity available to a company. Which would have the greater bottom line impact on your company—if your computers ran 10 percent faster or if your people performed 10 percent better?

Clearly there is high economic value to knowing which performance improvement programs are effective. Ineffective training programs can be dropped, saving the per day cost of training (often estimated at $500 to $2000 per day per participant, not counting the value of the participant time). That money can be reinvested in other more effective programs, spent on other business initiatives, or returned to investors or stockholders. There is solid evidence that effective performance products are directly responsible for increased income—sometimes far beyond the rate usually set as a reasonable return on the investment in plant or equipment. For example, McDonald and Smith (1995) reported that almost half of the 437 publicly traded companies they surveyed had performance management systems. Those companies who were focused on managing employee performance generated nearly 60 percent more return on equity, over 40 percent more return on assets, and a 7.9 percent total shareholder return versus zero percent for companies that did not focus on performance. The updated McKinsey study (Axelrod, Handfield-Jones, and Welsh 2001) also showed that the companies with the best talent management practices (top 20 percent) outperformed their industry's mean return to shareholders by 22 percent, a truly remarkable difference.

Some might argue that profitable companies can more easily afford a performance management focus. This implies, however, that profits cause companies to adopt performance management, not the other way around. It may be less painful to invest in human capital when an organization is profitable than when times are lean. Yet McDonald and Smith also tracked companies that had recently adopted a performance management system and found that, even in times of recession, they achieved an almost 25 percent increase in shareholder return.

Similar achievements are available to nearly all organizations. It is essential that change result from systematic analysis of the causes of performance gaps and be accompanied by necessary knowledge and skill changes and accompanying motivational adjustments. Sadly, examples of failed attempts to increase performance are even easier to find.

We Don't Have to Fail: A Medical Analogy

Perhaps the most annoying aspect of the frequency of failed attempts at performance improvement is that effective solutions are available for many performance problems. The job of testing the active ingredients in many of these products has already been done for us using the same scientific methods that inform other fields. So how do you access this information and use it to inform your decision-making processes? In a nutshell, we all need to use existing science-based information for product comparison and impact assessment as decisions are made to purchase, develop, and evaluate performance enhancing products and services. A medical analogy is helpful in explaining why science-based products are more effective.

We take medicine to attack the physical symptoms of illness and improve the way we feel. Medicines are composed of a specific combination of chemicals or active ingredients that target our symptoms and diseases. Medicines are tested extensively by pharmaceutical professionals for effectiveness, as well as for unintended side effects. In addition to the active ingredients, medicines contain lots of fillers, binders, coatings, color, flavoring, and other inert ingredients that have no biological or medical effect but make the medication easier or more appealing to use.

Medicines are prescribed to us by highly trained clinical professionals who have studied human biological systems, diseases of those systems, and the medicinal effects of chemicals on diseased systems. Our doctors also know our medical histories and, ideally, something about us as people. When we are sick, they examine our symptoms to diagnose our condition. They draw on their personal and cultural knowledge of us, select from an array of alternatives, and prescribe a medicine which is appropriate for both our disease and our unique biology, history, and lives. In selecting a treatment for us, our doctors draw on a very extensive body of medical and scientific research.

A long chain of cooperation exists among the many professionals who bring us medicine. This chain includes the chemists and biologists who make basic discoveries about human biology and biochemistry, the pharmacologists who design and test medicine, and the medical technicians who diagnose diseases and prescribe treatment for us. We expect that these professionals will employ the best available scientific data in their decisions, and that expectation is enforced by professional codes, standard protocols, and legal requirements.

Let's look at our organizations. Think of a performance problem as an illness within the organization. We use performance improvement strategies to remedy organizational problems related to people or to take advantage of opportunities to improve business results. Just as we now know that there are no universal tonics that cure everything from cancer to dandruff, there are no performance improvement tonics to fix all of our people problems from poor morale to weak skills. Performance improvement products need to be targeted at the root causes of performance problems. The products we buy should be designed by teams made up of professionals who understand science and those who know about organizations, their problems, and the specific actions that correct those problems.

While the analogy that connects medicine and performance interventions is far from perfect, there is an extensive body of social and behavioral science research about people, how they learn, and what motivates them to perform. Those of us in organizations who prescribe performance interventions must draw on this research to evaluate the effectiveness of these interventions and determine whether they are appropriate for our organization. To do otherwise is to waste time and money and to settle for hit-or-miss results.

Management Training: A Variable Return on Investment

In an all-too-rare evaluation of corporate training, one study showed very mixed results (Morrow et al. 1997). Of eleven corporate-wide programs studied, three did not provide enough impact to justify their cost—in other words, a waste of money. Two of the eleven programs (including a very expensive five-day executive seminar at a luxury mountain retreat) actually produced negative results. This means the participants performed *worse* after the training than before it. No details were given about what type of negative results occurred or their cost, yet similar findings can be seen in other studies (Clark 1989; Clark and Estes 1998, 1999).

Finally, the Morrow review found that the remaining six programs were highly cost-effective with rates of return from 16 percent (the approximate hurdle rate for investment in plant or equipment at many global corporations) to 492 percent. One simple program, developed in-house at low cost, had a rate of return of 1989 percent! This evidence refutes at least two extreme views of training—first, the belief on the part of some managers that *no* training is very worthwhile, and, second, that the best training must be slick, expensive, and include all the bells and whistles.

The decision to implement any performance improvement program must be made in the same way as any other business decision and viewed as a business investment. The evidence overwhelmingly supports the view that investing in improving employee performance generates income. It is likely that the benefit is considerably *underestimated* because of the negative impact of popular but carelessly chosen and defective programs (Clark 1989). When the financial impact of both positive and negative programs are summed, the negative programs subtract from the overall yield, and the result is often disappointing.

Avoiding the Snake Oil That Creates
Performance Losses or Has No Impact

A major challenge facing those responsible for developing the "human assets" in organizations is choosing among the motley crew of vendors who pitch a bewildering array of performance improvement products. Team-building, Myers-Briggs type profiling, empowerment, web-based training, multimedia, corporate culture transformation, job and work re-engineering, and management by storytelling are only a few of the huge variety of products and services offered to help us manage our opportunities and problems. New training and performance improvement companies appear every day, offering just-in-time, whizbang technologies that promise to manage our knowledge and skills for greater profits, motivate our people for improved service, and improve team communication and efficiency through electronic infrastructure. Our in-boxes overflow with slick brochures, our voice-mail is thick with honeyed sales pitches, our e-mail spams out a daily ration of E-ads, and our faxes grind out amazing performance improvement offers by the pound.

Do any of these things work? Do any of them do what they promise? How do you pick and choose? Their proponents claim they are working in successful organizations, that they provide the most recent technology, and that they are based on the work of world-renowned experts. So how can we lose? Why not simply pick the product that best matches our culture, or offers the lowest price, or is compatible with all the electronic gizmos our company just bought?

Not so fast. Why do so many of us notice little or no improvement from some of these products? Is it possible that some, perhaps many, of these performance enhancements are duds? Or that they can help or hurt an organization depending on how they are used? The following points illustrate some of the disturbing evidence about the downside of some very popular performance improvement products and services.

The Bad News about Some Popular Strategies

The health care industry uses the term *iatrogenic* to characterize a situation in which an attempt to help a patient makes the patient's health worse. An iatrogenic illness is caused by a physician who gives a patient the wrong treatment. Contrary to popular belief, there are clear iatrogenic problems in the performance improvement arena. Some of these problems are described next as examples of the risk we take when choosing improvement strategies.

- **Poorly designed or delivered training can make people perform worse after training than before training** (Clark 1989). All training is not helpful. Poorly designed training can depress performance in a couple of ways. One problem is that it can cause the scrambling of previously well-organized memory for a work-related topic. As a result, people are slower or unable to remember this information after training than they were before training. In this situation, an investment in training actually makes performance worse. In other cases, management team-building exercises have been found to increase destructive competition between management groups in the same organization (see the findings of Druckman and Bjork in chapter 2). These negative results refute the belief that any training will produce at least some positive results.

● **When used to evaluate performance improvement programs, reaction questionnaires or "smile sheets" often indicate the opposite of what happened** (Clark 1982). People often give very positive ratings to ineffective performance programs. Reaction forms ask people what they liked the most. What they like, however, is not always what helps them perform better. They may have liked the training because of the ease with which it was applied or the personality of the trainer. In these cases, people are affected by the less important aspects of a program and may rate it highly even if it made them less productive. Products that feel comfortable may not be challenging our current paradigms enough. For example, training programs have received high smile sheet ratings for client satisfaction, yet participants who are tested to see if they learned the course content show no learning gains. People report that they gained the most from a new approach when they may actually have gained little or lost ground.

The reverse can also happen. A successful program can be judged to be ineffective because it asks participants to change something very basic about their beliefs, expectations, and behavior. This counterintuitive result occurs, in part, because some interventions that make us more productive also challenge comfortable routine and our mental models of the world. This change process can make some of us uncomfortable. Some people do not like change in any form. Yet solving significant problems often requires change, and when we are feeling too comfortable we may choose the wrong medicine or too small a dosage. The result is like taking snake oil for a serious medical condition—the alcohol content may make you feel good for a while, but it does nothing to solve the real problem.

● **When experts design and present training in their area of expertise, they unintentionally give wrong information or fail to give complete information** (Clark and Estes 1996). The knowledge and skills of an expert, including the way they make decisions and solve problems, are highly automated and unconscious. They can't teach what they are not aware of doing even if they are committed to passing on what they do so well. Worse yet, experts are not aware that most of their knowledge and nearly all of their skills are unconscious. Yet almost all of them believe that they are giving accurate and complete information to trainees. Since most training in organizations is based on content derived from interviewing experts, this is a major problem. We discuss this phenomenon in more detail in chapter 4.

- **According to independent assessments and research, the popular Myers-Briggs Type Indicator (MBTI) is neither reliable nor valid** (Pittenger 1993a, 1993b). The MBTI is often used to match people who are compatible or to tailor interactions or management strategies to people's different styles or types. The research evidence described on page 10 indicates that the MBTI does not measure the same types in the same way each time it is used (like a yardstick made of a stretchy material), nor does it accurately predict people's work behavior. People usually get different scores or profiles on the MBTI each time they take it. Simply being aware that individuals have different styles and that there is value in accommodating those individual differences in the workplace probably produces most of the positive results imputed to the MBTI.

- **When the performance of work teams is evaluated as a group, rather than evaluating individual members of the group, individual productivity declines significantly** (Williams and Karau 1991; Karau and Williams 1993, 1995). This phenomenon, called social loafing, occurs when group members reduce their individual effort, believing that their contribution won't be missed. It also appears that when managers add more members to groups to increase their output, individual performance falls even farther if group members do not believe that their individual contributions are being assessed.

- **More than 60 percent of the organizational change strategies undertaken by companies are quickly abandoned** (Druckman and Bjork 1991, 1994; Druckman et al. 1997). The U.S. National Academy of Sciences extensively surveyed research on organizational change and concluded that few organizational change strategies are sustained. This research confirms the common experience we have at work: senior managers are smitten with a consultant's or guru's promises, and the whole organization is pitched into the frenzy of implementing a program. In two or three months, after lots of hard work and effort taken away from other projects, it becomes apparent that the program is not producing the promised results. It is quickly and unceremoniously buried with its predecessors. The Academy members who conducted the review expressed serious reservations about the quality of the change strategies being used in many large organizations. Most of these consultants do not intend to cheat or bamboozle their customers; the problem is that their remedies are ineffective—there are no active ingredients or the active ingredients are not appropriate for this organization and situation.

WHY ARE MANY RESEARCHERS NEGATIVE ABOUT THE MYERS-BRIGGS TYPE INDICATOR (MBTI)?

One of the most interesting disputes in performance research surrounds the very popular MBTI. The test is often used for career counseling, to adjust working relationships, and to "type" organizations. The National Research Council estimates that just over a decade ago, nearly two million people a year were taking the MBTI (Druckman and Bjork 1991). That number has likely increased over time. Advocates of the test point out that it is reliable (corrected split-half and alpha reliability scores range from .75 to .85, an acceptable level for a "trait" test). The MBTI also seems to have construct validity, since experts agree that it represents both the Jungian concepts it's intended to measure and some of the sixteen types as they are defined in other psychological research publications. The test has obvious face validity since most of the people who take it believe that the results are accurate and reflect their own experiences.

So why are so many researchers upset about this test? Why does the National Research Council of the National Academy of Sciences conclude that "the lack of a supportive research foundation for the MBTI leads the committee to recommend that the instrument not be used ... until its validity is supported by research" (Druckman and Bjork 1991, 100)? Why did a more recent review published in a top research journal conclude that "there is no convincing evidence that knowledge of type is a reliable or valid predictor of important behavioral conditions....The patterns of data do not suggest that there is reason to believe that there are sixteen unique types of personality..." (Pittenger 1993, 483) and suggest that there are "ethical issues...with respect to specific uses of the test" (482)? Answering these questions is complex, yet here are four of the reasons measurement researchers and the National Research Council reject the test:

1. **Positive research on the MBTI tends to be poorly designed and published by the same group that sells the test. More objective reviews are negative.**

   Reviews of MBTI studies (Thayer 1988) have identified a pattern of inconsistent and incomplete data and incorrect statistical analyses (no baselines, subjects are often aware of the hypotheses being tested, no overall tests of significance before detailed comparisons are made). Attempts by mainstream psychologists to replicate a number of the positive research findings reported by advocates have too often failed (Druckman and Bjork 1991). Most of the positive studies have been published by Journals of the Center for the Applications of Psychological Type, and few studies appear in mainstream measurement or psychological journals where peer review is required.

2. **While the overall reliability of the test seems adequate, the specific types on the MBTI are not reliable.**

   The MBTI is a "types" test, not a "trait" test. Types tests are required to establish that individuals belong in one single type and that people do not change type quickly or easily. (For a discussion of reliability standards, refer to the APA's "Standards for educational and psychological testing" cited at the end of this chapter.) The National Research Council reported that between 60 and 88 percent of the people in about a dozen large groups who took the MBTI in controlled studies changed their type classification within five weeks of taking the test (Druckman and Bjork 1991, 97). Since reliability is a necessary condition for all types of validity, this consistent finding is very distressing. It is questionable how anyone can apply knowledge from an instrument that identifies types that change over a short period of time.

3. **The MBTI is popular for vocational and career advancement counseling, but no evidence has been presented suggesting that it either discriminates between occupations or predicts performance in occupations.**

Studies reported in mainstream psychological and educational journals report that for many occupations, the MBTI does not accurately discriminate between either people in those occupations or their performance. For example, the National Research Council reports that while about 12 percent of elementary teachers in the United States are ESFJ's, "the same percentage of a random sample of U.S. women are also ESFJ's," and that there is "no evidence...presented on relationships [between MBTI types and work] performance in...occupations" (Druckman and Bjork 1991, 98). They also described validity reviews in twenty studies where the I-E scale seemed to be solid but the S-N and T-F scales were very weak. While the I-E scale was solid, other measures of this trait were even better. There is no evidence that the test measures sixteen distinct types. More important is the National Research Council's conclusion that most of the types described in the test should be tapped by more solid tests.

4. **The value of the MBTI may be in increased sensitivity to individual and group differences or for career counseling, but no solid research has been conducted on these issues.**

Friends who have taken the MBTI claim that it might help raise the consciousness of individuals in work environments who implicitly believe that everyone is more or less like them. Being aware that other people have different values and behavior patterns—and that there is value in accommodating those differences in the workplace and in work processes—may produce very positive results for organizations. Yet, as the National Academy notes, "neither the gains in sensitivity nor the impact of those gains on performance have been documented by research. Nor has the instrument been validated in a long-term study of successful and unsuccessful careers. Lacking such evidence, it is a curiosity why the instrument is used so widely, particularly in organizations" (Druckman and Bjork 1991, 99).

- **The choice of newer electronic media for training does not influence learning, but may make new knowledge and skills less expensive than traditional media** (Clark 1994, 2001). New communication technologies *can* make information and training available more quickly and less expensively to more people; the savings of time and money can be very impressive. However, some people advocate the move to computer-based Internet and Intranet training and job support based on the view that presenting knowledge and skills via computer is more effective. This argument is deeply flawed. People learn better from well-designed materials and solid, carefully selected learning methods, whether the learning takes place online, in a classroom, from self-paced materials, or paper job aids. Putting poor training online does not magically transform it into effective training. Putting good training online does not make it better training, though it may significantly reduce expenses.

- **Employee empowerment strategies can have both positive AND negative effects, depending on the culture in which they are used** (Clark 1998). Many people are more motivated when empowerment strategies allow them to participate in deciding *how* they do a job (but not *what* job they do). These strategies are called by various names—"Quality Circles," "Leaderless Teams," and "Self-Directed Work Groups" are a few examples. However, in some organizational cultures, giving people control of how they do their jobs backfires and causes lowered motivation and increased employee turnover. In some organizational cultures, people are more motivated by a strong managerial presence, and empowerment is seen as disruptive and interfering with an effective manager.

- **Some competency-based approaches do not work.** A significant number of performance improvement vendors now emphasize "competency-based systems." Advocates of competency-based systems analyze your operation and suggest a master list of the performance competencies necessary to ensure success. A possible outcome would be to require that people be able to: "Manage profit and loss, control expenses, and set and manage financial goals." Who could disagree? If high level and abstract competencies help you get support for the specific work goals that drive performance, they are positive. If general goals replace concrete, specific, and timely goals, they can be both distracting and destructive. The competencies you need from people will change as business goals change. General competencies are only the beginning and cannot serve as adequate work goals for teams or individuals. There is no research or evaluation evidence to support the idea that identifying important general competencies by reasoning about goals make any difference in performance. What is necessary is a more comprehensive approach such as the one we'll describe in chapter 2.

Where Does Your Organization Score?

A "Yes" answer to the following questions indicates a positive move in the direction of assuring that tested products are being selected and untested products are avoided when tested products are available. A "No" answer indicates an opportunity for improvement and a need for the information in this book. A "Don't know" answer is an opportunity to learn important information about your organization.

WHERE DOES YOUR ORGANIZATION SCORE?

Does your organization require pre-purchase information about the research support for performance products and services?

YES _____ NO _____ Don't Know _____

Have you noticed advertising copy for performance products describing the results of scientific evaluation of the product?

YES _____ NO _____ Don't Know _____

Do any of the people who try to sell you performance products describe the results of scientifically designed comparison studies with competing products?

YES _____ NO _____ Don't Know _____

Do you or anyone in your organization routinely ask vendors about the research support for a product or service you are considering?

YES _____ NO _____ Don't Know _____

When people in your organization design performance improvement strategies, do they consult performance research for guidance on what approaches work best?

YES _____ NO _____ Don't Know _____

Recommendations and Result Transfer

Some of the most popular performance products may never have been effective, even though they have attracted strong advocates. This can be true even in organizations where assessment of a new product is routine. Most organizations do not systematically evaluate performance products. Instead they give out reaction forms or smile sheets, which, as discussed earlier, often misrepresent the program's success. When reactions gathered by the smile sheets are positive, managers feel confident that the product worked, and so they implement it widely and recommend it to others. Personal recommendations from colleagues are a very powerful incentive to choose the same performance improvement strategy for your organization.

Thus failures are unintentionally reported to others as a success and accompanied with a "Try it! It worked for us." Successes can be reported as a failure or a "Pass on this one" recommendation. Since it is reasonable to believe that the people giving the recommendation have already tested the product, adopters feel less pressure to evaluate its use in a new setting. This compounds the problem and paves the way for the product to continue to receive inaccurate reviews from our peers. This is how fads begin and why "it worked for us" peer suggestions need to be checked carefully before being adopted.

However, regardless of whether a program is really successful, it is not always reasonable to assume that positive *or* negative results will be replicated in a different environment. Just as medication types, dosages, and delivery media often have to be adjusted for people with different body weight and metabolism, the performance solutions that succeed for one person or group may fail for others or vice versa. People differ in personality, style, expertise, ability, and values. Organizations differ in many ways including culture and mission. While some performance products may work once in a specific organization, there is no guarantee that they will work in a different organization. In some cases, the same product may not succeed the second time it is used in the same organization. Performance specialists call this "transfer failure," which may be another name for our own brand of iatrogenic illness (Stolevitch 1999).

This lack of clear results is demoralizing. The bitter irony of this tragedy is that our failure to engineer and accurately evaluate performance products comes at a time when research and development of human performance improvement strategies are achieving their greatest gains in this century. At the moment, the gap between what we have learned from the past two decades of research on human performance and what we actually do in modern organizations is embarrassingly and dangerously wide. Studies by the National Academy of Sciences, the National Research Council, and many blue ribbon scientific and industry study groups reported during the 1990s reach the conclusion that we are not taking advantage of what we have learned in performance research (Druckman and Bjork 1991, 1994; Druckman et al. 1997).

Advantages of Science-Based Products and Services

Here are the potential benefits of a science-based performance product selection and development system:

- Achieve key organizational goals by improving the effectiveness of people.

- Focus interventions on the key drivers of superior performance and only those critical few.

- Save time and money by selecting only reliable and valid products.

- Get a better fit for your needs when adjusting off-the-shelf products.

- Solve performance problems and reduce unintended side effects.

- Get the right data to know what's working and what is not.

Many people will wonder why the information in this book is not more widely known and appreciated. In fact, many managers simply do not trust performance enhancement. In their experience, these products seldom have visible impact. Performance consultants often hear stories about people who come back from training and either were not trained to do what is necessary, do not use what they were trained to do, or are unable to apply it at work. Motivational programs in sales and productivity sometimes result in a short-term increase in enthusiasm, but are often long-term duds. Others tend to use these products and services out of desperation when faced with an expensive problem (and very little time to solve it), as good luck charms when major changes are planned, or as part of employee entitlements such as vacation and health benefits.

Yet performance change is not a punishment, a reward, or a feel-good pill. It is not part of the expense of employee benefits. When it works, it helps to achieve organizational goals, and the expense is part of the investment side of doing business. When it fails, it can make things considerably worse and damage our ability to survive. Thus there is a big incentive to find cost-effective solutions.

Opinion Versus Fact: The Time Problem

There is too much to learn and too little time. The amount of time training and performance improvement professionals have available to master a complex and sometimes conflicting performance research literature is even more limited today than it was a decade ago. Reports of research contain language that is specialized and difficult to understand without extensive education and training. Since researchers disagree, many people get the impression that performance sciences are opinion and that all opinions are equally valid.

Recent arguments in universities about the role of science and technology in society have placed further strains on science education. Some otherwise educated people argue that science is not an appropriate way to understand human behavior. These people often paint science as an authoritarian system that emphasizes quantity over quality. Some believe that human performance cannot or should not be studied scientifically.

Our view of these arguments is simply that they are wrong. If an alternative to scientific method can be found that more accurately and efficiently forecasts the success of performance solutions in organizations and reliably identifies products that do not work, we will eagerly adopt it and encourage others to adopt it also. While our individual and collective understanding of science is imperfect, the

---

MISCONCEPTIONS ABOUT SCIENCE-BASED PERFORMANCE PRODUCTS

Most people have a number of beliefs about the benefits and drawbacks of using science to evaluate and select performance products. Some of the misconceptions that cause problems are:

● **Using scientific test information is too complex. Only scientists and people with advanced training can use scientific evidence to select performance products.**

People with no scientific training use scientific test information to make product decisions all the time. Have you ever changed your eating or exercise habits because of news reports based on medical or nutritional research? In the past few years, most people have changed their eating, drinking, or smoking habits considerably as a result of scientific research reports. Would you buy a new car without checking the results of tests reported in reviews such as *Consumer Reports* if they were available to you? Car manufacturers have become much more concerned about lower ratings on their models by both government and independent testing services, precisely because those results directly influence sales.

● **Checking the scientific evidence for performance solutions takes too much time.**

The general planning rule is that the amount of front end time you should spend analyzing before acting should be either a) enough to get whatever test information you need to make an informed decision or b) approximately 25 percent of the time available to select or design and implement a performance solution. If you have one day to get something started, spend the first quarter of that day looking for test data. Time spent choosing a solid product protects against failure. How much time do you now spend checking out a new car before you buy it? Doesn't it seem reasonable to put the same

cumulative social and economic benefits of science and the technologies it generates are obvious, tangible, and impressive.

It is not necessary to fully understand performance research and development in order to select effective vendors of products or services. Few of us have the expertise to understand the subtle issues in medical research on diet or exercise. It is, however, very necessary to invest scarce resources in products that survive scientifically impartial tests. This book is a resource for how to use scientific knowledge to make better decisions about performance.

The next chapter will discuss the first step to improving performance: setting business goals and determining the distance between those goals and current

amount of analysis into a business decision and treat it as if it were your money and your family? What is the cost of making a mistake that causes performance to stay the same? Remember that if a hastily chosen solution fails, you will have wasted 100 percent of your money and still have missed your deadline.

● **My manager does not ask for this kind of information. Why should I bother?**

Your manager may feel the same way many people do before they get the opportunity to analyze the situation and realize that there is a more cost-effective way to make these decisions. This issue is probably not the only one where you will have the opportunity to help your manager understand the benefits of a new approach.

● **Some performance interventions, such as team building, do not need to be specifically evaluated because they are just generally good for an organization.**

These interventions promise to improve overall performance, rather than solve a particular problem (suggesting, for example, that learning to play chess or program a computer makes you a better thinker). Alas, there are no "silver bullets" or general "tonics" for performance improvement. Learning to play chess makes you a better chess player, but does not really make significant improvement to your computer programming skills, your financial analysis acumen, or your rapport with colleagues (unless they are also chess players). If you want to develop one of those skills, you must study and deliberately practice that skill. Training, coaching, and job redesign are all specific interventions targeted at specific organizational opportunities or problems, just as medicines are targeted at specific diseases and bodily systems. There are no general "performance tonics." Tonics went out with snake oil hucksters. Yet there are features of successful programs that can effectively be targeted to specific problems in specific organizational contexts.

performance. We begin with the way that goals are set and communicated. This section also describes which types of goals improve work performance the most. The chapter will then describe how to select services and products that help you determine the size and causes of current gaps between your business goals and the current employee work performance.

Additional Resources on Performance Research

Topic: *Scientific Method for Solving Practical Problems—The Science to Technology Process*

American Psychological Association, American Educational Research Association & National Council on Measurement in Education. 1985. *Standards for educational and psychological testing*. Washington, D.C.: American Psychological Association.

Crichton, Michael. 1999. Ritual abuse, hot air, and missed opportunities. *Science* 284 (9 April): 238-240.

Christensen, C. 1997. *The innovator's dilemma: When new technologies cause great firms to fail*. Cambridge: Harvard Business School Press.

Clark, Richard E., and Fred Estes. 1998. Technology or craft: What are we doing? *Educational Technology* 38, no. 5: 5-11.

———. 1999. The development of authentic educational technologies. *Educational Technology* 39, no. 2: 5-16.

———. 2000. A proposal for the collaborative development of authentic performance technology. *Performance Improvement* 39, no. 4: 48-53.

Druckman, Daniel, Jerome E. Singer, and Harold Van Cott, eds. 1997. *Enhancing organizational performance*. Washington, D.C.: National Academy Press.

Estes, Fred, and Richard E. Clark. 1999. Authentic Educational Technology: The lynchpin between theory and practice. *Educational Technology* 39, no. 6: 5-13.

Gilbert, Thomas F. 1996. *Human competence: Engineering worthy performance, tribute edition*. Washington, D.C.: International Society for Performance Improvement.

Norman, Donald A. 1988. *The psychology of everyday things*. New York: Basic Books.

Resnick, Lauren B. 1987. *Education and learning to think*. Washington, D.C.: National Academy Press.

Schwartz, Peter. 1991. *The art of the long view: Planning for the future in an uncertain world.* New York: Doubleday.

Stolevitch, Harold. 1997. Introduction to the special issue on transfer of training—transfer of learning. *Performance Improvement Quarterly* 10, no. 2:5-6.

2

Setting Performance Goals That Support Organizational Goals

ORGANIZATIONS NEED TO BE GOAL-DRIVEN, and currently, most performance or work goal systems are not tied to an organization's business goals. This chapter will show you how to remedy that problem by focusing on how to establish business goals, set specific performance goals, measure the gap between current achievement and desired performance goal levels, and determine the cost-benefit of closing each gap.

The next chapters will describe research-tested ways to identify the causes of performance gaps through gap analysis and implement the appropriate performance solutions. Gap analysis diagnoses the human causes behind performance gaps. But without a clear picture of the goals we are trying to reach, gap analysis is futile. Figure 2.1 describes the plan for the book.

The Importance of Setting Goals

Effective performance improvement must start with

Figure 2.1

Turning Research Into Results *Process Model*

STEP 1	STEP 2	STEP 3
Identify key **business goals.** (Chapter 2)	Identify individual **performance goals.** (Chapter 2)	Determine **performance gaps.** (Chapter 2)

STEP 5A

Identify **knowledge/skill** solutions and implement. (Chapter 4)

STEP 6	STEP 5B	STEP 4
Evaluate results, tune system and revise goals. (Chapter 7)	Identify **motivation** solutions and implement. (Chapter 5)	**Analyze gaps** to determine causes. (Chapter 3)

STEP 5C

Identify **organizational** process and material solutions and implement. (Chapter 6)

© 2002 CEP Press

clearly understood work goals (Bandura 1997) and accurate analysis of the cause of the gaps between current and desired performance (Gilbert 1996; Rummler and Brache 1995; Locke and Latham 1990). A performance or work goal is a description of tasks or objectives that individuals and teams must accomplish according to specific deadlines and criteria. Effective performance goals cascade or follow from organizational or business goals. The gap between desired and actual performance must be assessed and closed if organizational goals are to be achieved. Alignment between the organization and its employees begins with compatible goal structures. Without this initial step, all other attempts to improve performance are like traveling in the dark to an unknown destination through dangerous territory. The ultimate objective for performance improvement is that it must support the larger goals of the organization. So the first task is to be aware of the business goals you will support if you solve the performance problem you are facing. Every member of each work team should have a very clear and specific description of their own performance goals, how to know when they are (or are not) achieving those goals, and the business reason for each goal. The sidebar on page 24 describes an argument for the cost-benefit of goal setting first developed by Thomas Gilbert (1996) and its impact on "worthy performance."

Too many organizations fail to make the connection between high-level organizational goals and specific team/individual work goals. While goal setting may not be an exciting task, it is often the missing link in performance improvement. Job descriptions are seldom adequate sources of performance goals since they tend to be fixed, general, or vague. Organizational goals must be flexible to reflect changing business conditions and specific enough to meet the need for day-to-day guidance. The work goals managers assign to people must directly support evolving organizational goals.

Without clear and specific performance goals, people tend to focus on tasks that help advance their careers instead of helping the organization achieve its goals. Some human resources and training professionals also tend not to think of goal setting or goal identification as their job and so tend to ignore this step. As to whether people should decide their own work goals, some believe that unless people are involved in setting their own goals, they will not be motivated to achieve them. This is a misconception. Even the "employee empowerment" movement of the 1980s and 1990s did not recommend that people choose their own work goals. The idea was to motivate people by engaging them in discussions about *how* they do their work—not *what* work they must do. Locke and Latham (1990) have conducted research on this issue for many years and present compelling evidence that people can easily accept and be motivated to do their best with assigned work goals.

Research on work goals strongly suggests that the types of work goals selected and the way they are communicated to people are both vital concerns. The researchers who have devoted the most time to examining this issue are Locke and Latham (1990), and one of the most famous of all American psychologists, Albert Bandura (1997). Studies of work goals conclude that employees do not have to participate in work goal setting in order to give strong commitment to the goal they have been assigned. In cases where participatory goal setting is not possible, value for the goal is enhanced if people perceive the person or team who assign the goal to meet some or all of the following characteristics:

- A legitimate, trusted authority,

- With an inspiring vision that reflects a convincing rationale for the goal,

- Who expects outstanding performance from everyone,

- Gives ownership to individuals and teams for specific tasks and accomplishments,

- Expresses confidence in individual and team capabilities,

WORTHY PERFORMANCE PROVIDES COST-EFFECTIVE SUPPORT FOR BUSINESS GOALS.

Most of us assume that performance problems are caused by people who avoid or resist work, and/or do not work hard enough. In fact, many performance problems occur when people are working very hard. Some of the hardest working people we've encountered were investing their best effort in failing organizations. The prospect of failure is a very negative motivator, but it often serves to focus attention and encourage very hard work. Occasionally, that hard work does not succeed, and an organization, or some part of an organization, fails. A key point about performance is that to understand it, a person must realize that all behavior at work is not productive or valuable. Thomas Gilbert (1996), a clear thinker about human competence, pointed out convincingly that performance is efficient work behavior that supports valued organizational goals. He suggests the following metric to understand worthy performance:

$$W = A/B$$

where W = worthy [effective or useful] performance supporting business goals; A = the business value of the accomplishment; and B = the cost of the accomplishment. So where the value of the business-focused accomplishment A is more than the cost of the behavior B, we have achieved productive and "worthy" performance. For example, suppose your company can save $200,000 a year by investing $50,000 a year in quality training. Using the formula above, the value of the worthy performance is 4.0 (W= $200,000/$50,000), mathematically equivalent to a return on investment (ROI) of 300% [($200,000 savings – $50,000 cost of training)/$50,000 cost of training]. On the other hand, if the training cost $200,000 each year and the annual cost saving was $50,000, then the training is not productive for the organization (W= .25), as W is less than 1.0. In that case, assuming the total business costs and benefits to the company are all included and correctly calculated, this training should not be done.

- Provides feedback focused on task performance and on gaps between expected and observed behavior (not on the faults of the person or team), and

- Gives recognition for success as well as corrective suggestions for mistakes.

Work Goal Format and Structure—C³ Goals

In addition to the qualities of a trusted manager who provides a challenging vision, strong expectations, and clear feedback, the way work goals are structured have a

To understand worthy performance, we must know something about an organization's business goals and be able to translate those goals so that everyone in an organization understands and knows how to achieve them. The more we ignore or guess at these goals, the less effective we will be in supporting excellent performance.

Work Goals Must Be Carefully Set and Constantly Monitored and Changed
The purpose of work goals is to support the achievement of business goals. The more that markets change, the more that business goals must evolve. In *The Innovator's Dilemma: When New Technologies Cause Great Firms to Fail*, Clayton Christensen (1997) discusses the concept of the value network, which is the web of customers' wants and needs and competitors' value propositions. Companies that do not stay in close touch with their customers fall by the wayside. For example, Digital Equipment Corporation created the minicomputer market, but missed the personal computer market and ended up being acquired by Compaq. When business goals are modified to accommodate changes in customer demands, the work goals of employees must accommodate those changes.

Many formerly successful organizations have either failed or taken a major hit because they did not modify business goals to reflect market changes. Organizations such as IBM were on most lists in the 1970s and, more recently, Unisys and Sears. Those companies learned this lesson too late to prevent major losses.

How many organizations have been hurt because their performance goals do not reflect business goals? There has not been enough discussion of the importance of changing work goals to reflect the rapid evolution of business goals over time and communicating those changes to employees. What use is modifying our business goals to reflect changing markets unless changes are clearly communicated? People who continue to do their job in the same way in the face of rapid changes in business goals unintentionally cause deterioration in their own performance. Their performance deteriorates because the value of what they do diminishes.

major influence on their impact and acceptance. The best work goals are C³ Goals:

- **Concrete** (clear, easily understandable, and measurable);

- **Challenging** (doable but very difficult); and

- **Current** (short-term daily or weekly goals are more motivating than longer-term monthly or annual goals).

There is solid evidence from research that work motivation depends, in large part, on the availability and quality of work goals. The reason for this finding is that without clear goals, it is not possible to know whether we are succeeding or failing.

Goal Setting Pitfalls

One of the biggest hazards of goal setting arises because people fear "analysis paralysis," or overanalyzing problems to the extent that no action is taken. As a result of this fear, they make the mistake of engaging in impulsive action (deciding without an adequate analysis) in an attempt to keep problems from causing more serious consequences. With the problem framed as "Should I analyze or act?" too many people choose not to conduct more than a momentary analysis in order to act quickly. This is a very destructive way to frame the issue. Common results of impulsive action when setting goals are setting "stretch goals" (which cause motivation problems), and/or setting too many goals (causing thrashing). We will discuss stretch goals and thrashing later in this chapter.

Each of us could cite case after case of a hasty training solution put in place when the root cause was an incomplete process, a missing tool, a resistance to using skills, or an unaligned organization. In one memorable case, a service business wanted to convert a paper time sheet used by its professional staff to electronic format. Senior managers, who were under pressure to get it done yesterday, decreed that there would be a training course without thinking about what, if anything, would need to be learned. Though trainers realized, after rapid analysis, that the problem was motivational, they were still instructed to provide training. The end result: a quick and expensive training program, angry middle managers, surprised and truculent trainees, trainers facing hostility, and a problem that still wasn't solved. It would be great if this example of how impulsive action failed and led to a cycle of further impulsive and futile management reactions was a rare event in business, but unfortunately, that's not the case.

How do we balance the need for quick action with the absolute need for analysis? Our suggestion is to find ways to make quick diagnoses when you have very little time—a strategy we call the 25-75 solution—devote 25 percent of your time to analysis no matter how much time you have to deliver a solution—and give 75 percent of your time to design and implementation. The next chapter on gap analysis discusses this issue in greater depth.

Stretch Goals: The term "stretch goal" has very different meanings for different managers. Most people who use the term "stretch" mean "to give people an impossible goal and they may achieve the impossible." Very challenging but possible-to-achieve stretch goals are highly motivating. However, when stretch goals are perceived to be impossible, people stop trying or find creative ways to avoid them. The challenge for those who set goals is to find a way to take people beyond their current comfort zones, but set the bar at a point that is within reach with maximum effort.

Thrashing: Another common problem with goal-setting is the temptation to generate too many goals for everyone. Goals are absolutely necessary to direct effort. Yet many organizations seem tempted to set a large number of top priority goals, leaving people running in too many directions trying to follow too many directives. This situation has been called thrashing—a term derived from the early mainframe days of computers to describe a system shuffling between too many tasks and accomplishing no productive work.

Since the effort required to achieve any one priority goal can vary enormously, it is not possible to suggest a specific number of goals that people can handle with maximum effort. People have a limited amount of attentional and mental "bandwidth"; even the brightest and most motivated people have a limited capacity. Current evidence suggests people can think about approximately three to five new chunks or items at once, and that number decreases as stress increases. People are only able to invest inadequate and shallow effort in each item when forced to distribute effort over too many priorities. They need to focus their attentions on a limited number of challenging goals. When setting goals, the trick is to limit them to only those few that will result in the maximum business impact. There has to be enough wood behind the arrow for key goals to be accomplished.

Do You Need a Business-Driven Performance Goal System? A Checklist

Does your organization develop and communicate its business goals to everyone? Are business goals translated into work goals for different divisions, teams, and individuals so that everyone knows their own part in achieving the greater objective? Tackle the quick checklist in figure 2.2 to see if you need to consider a new approach to setting work goals.

A "Yes" answer to any of the following questions indicates a positive move in the direction of setting, communicating, and modifying work goals. A "No" answer to any of the following indicates the need for improvement in your work goal system. If you are not absolutely certain about the answers to these questions, circle "No."

Figure 2.2

Business-Driven Performance Goal System Checklist

Does your organization:

- Have a system for developing and modifying business goals?   Yes   No
- Communicate business goals to everyone in the organization?   Yes   No
- Provide employees with individual or team work goals?   Yes   No
- Link work goals clearly to the organization's business goals?   Yes   No
- Provide feedback to employees on their progress towards work goals?   Yes   No

© 2002 CEP Press

Setting Business Goals

Every business has the goal to make a profit. Yet this very general objective must be translated into more specific goals that reflect the unique opportunities, capabilities, and challenges facing each business and every individual and team in the business. Organizational goals often result from a vision of where and how a company must develop in order to survive in a changing economy. Many organizations generate their annual business goals by benchmarking exercises in which they identify and try to equal or surpass the industry leader's current performance. Many of the best organizations have adopted organizational goals that go beyond their business plans and reflect their commitment to add value to their community, nation, or world. Kaufman (1996, 2000) has constructed a three-level approach to strategic thinking based on the idea that business planning must begin with a vision of the business's impact on society and the economy as a whole. Kaufman argues that sound business strategies start at the societal level and cascade down through the organizational level to the individual and work team level. When businesses neglect this macroeconomic systems view and focus only on quarterly profits, two negative consequences occur. First, they miss major, epochal changes in markets (Drucker

1999; Hamel and Prahalad 1994) or in technology (Christensen 1997) and get trounced by smarter and nimbler competitors. Second, they miss the unintended side effects of their business practices, such as poor toxic waste disposal practices contaminating groundwater and causing public health problems, or increasing exploitive child labor practices while seeking cheaper manufacturing costs in developing nations. Once identified, these organizational goals are communicated in mission statements and annual development plans. It is necessary to analyze all organizational goals, including business goals, to ensure that they are cost-effective.

The next section describes a procedure for setting business goals and then describes a way to connect them to individual and team performance expectations. We describe how to select external consultants who will perform the procedure for you using current research on performance goal setting. There is an entire literature on business strategy and business planning which is not reproduced here, though we provide some key references. The critical point is that businesses have extensive procedures for deciding whether to invest in new plants and equipment, to reduce inventory or cash levels, or to determine the cost-effectiveness of stock versus debt financing. These same procedures, however, are rarely applied to human performance initiatives. In order to buy a new computer system for $100,000, a manager would probably need to prepare an extensive business case, including cost justification, for senior management's review. Yet this same manager may be allowed to spend much more than $100,000 on human performance initiatives with only cursory explanation or review.

How can this be? First, business investment planning procedures were developed using accounting practices which only valued physical or financial resources. For all the talk today about the importance of human capital, the accounting profession is still wrestling with how to value human capital and intellectual property. As a result, these very real assets are often undervalued and given too little attention in strategy and planning. Second, the costs of human performance initiatives are often obscure or unmeasured. Training budgets might be distributed to individual managers across the company with no business-wide perspective or consolidation. Alternately, in costing a training initiative, managers may only include the hard dollar costs of instructors, materials, and travel and lodging costs. Unless the value of each employee's time is considered along with the effectiveness of the intervention, then the costs are understated. For knowledge businesses, the dollar costs of professional staff time is a major expense.

Setting and Analyzing Benchmarked Business Goals

Step 1: List the areas where you will set business goals and describe the indicators you will use to determine the achievement of each goal.

Step 2: Benchmark and quantify the industry leader's achievement in each business area.

Step 3: Quantify your organization's current achievement in each business area.

Step 4: Compute the gap by subtracting your achievement from the industry leader.

Step 5: Determine the economic benefit of closing the gap.

Step 6: Identify individual and team goals that will close each gap.

WHEN IMPULSIVELY SET PERFORMANCE GOALS HURT AN ORGANIZATION

The scientific study of goal setting in work settings is one of the most developed areas of performance research. A consistent finding in goal setting research is that most people in organizations report that they are not provided with clear performance goals. Where performance goals are provided, people often do not understand the connection between their goals and the larger business goals of the organization. Where clear, business focused performance goals are not provided, people develop their own personal work priorities and occasionally they develop their own goals. These individually-set priorities and goals may not support the business and, in some cases, may unintentionally work against the organization (Locke and Latham 1990). In their classic book, *Improving Performance: How to Manage the White Space on the Organization Chart*, Rummler and Brache (1995) demonstrate how organizational goals must be linked to business processes which must in turn be linked to individual jobs in order to manage effectively and to achieve organizational goals. To extend Rummler and Brache's rephrasing of a Chinese proverb, the negative impact of a lack of clear goals is that most people say to themselves: "If we don't know where we are going, any job priorities and goals will get us there, *so we might as well make up our own!*"

For example, the U.S. National Academy of Sciences surveyed all of the research on organizational team building strategies (Druckman and Bjork 1994). The performance improvement methods they surveyed attempted to get members of work teams to bond, collaborate, compete effectively and work efficiently toward common goals. When the Academy released its findings, it was not surprising to learn that many of the most popular team-building programs had succeeded in

STEP 1   List business goal areas and describe achievement indicators.

Let's assume that our business, General Products, is setting its business goals. There are a number of ways to choose strategic goals (see approaches suggested by Morrisey 1996; Schwartz 1991; and Porter 1998, 1980). The mission statement of General Products clearly reflects the goal of leading its industry sector in all areas. After discussion, managers will list all areas of the business and the types of indicators that can be quantified and used to measure achievement. Profit and loss is expressed in financial terms. Since everyone will eventually tie performance to profit and loss, goals must be quantitative. Your job at this stage is to find accurate quantities for each goal. Below are some examples of successful measures of business goal indicators.

increasing collaboration and cooperation between team members. Team building is often forced upon divisions in an organization without a clear idea of its business need or its impact on the larger organization.

What was surprising was that many of the "built" teams in the National Academy survey were competing in a nearly suicidal fashion with other teams in the same organization. They were doing everything possible to make their own team look good by making other teams in the same organization look bad. In our experience of this phenomenon, files are lost or destroyed, e-mail messages are deleted, fake memos are written to misdirect another team's efforts. Even in organizations without active sabotage, past a certain point, increasing the cohesiveness of individual teams decreased necessary collaboration among teams. When this happens along functional lines, for example between sales and manufacturing, some team building exercises can exacerbate traditional organizational tensions. In short, the behavior of the teams fit the goals supported by the team-building exercise, but the consequence of the new behavior was very destructive to the business goals of the larger organization. It is certainly the case that such goals would not be approved if there was a chance that they would conflict with business goals. The cost of achieving conflicting goals eliminates any benefit and the performance is negative. As a result, the National Academy of Sciences warned organizations to be cautious with team-building exercises. For example, consider team building along business process lines rather than within purely functional units. This type of misdirected behavior at work happens in many contexts. A lot of behavior, even new behavior gained from training at work, does not necessarily lead to a positive result. Everyone should ask about the organizational benefit and cost of work behavior. Analyze the total system and consider the impact of unintended side effects.

Business Goal Areas and Indicators

- Accounting data: Actual or percent estimates of sales, expenses, or profits.

- Market share: Select one industry standard for total market and divide by sales.

- Quality: Usually in terms of product characteristics, such as number of defects.

- Service Surveys: Based on percent of "bad" or "good" responses on customer surveys.

Presumably all divisions and functions in a business matrix would be included in this exercise. The choice of indicators must be consistent with both the data considered important by the business and those monitored by the industry. After listing all functions and the indicators to be used to measure progress, the next step is to benchmark the industry leaders.

 Benchmark and quantify the industry leader's achievement in each business area.

General Products' management team decides that their goal is to match or exceed the industry leader in certain key target areas. The next step is to get the benchmark data for those target areas. These numbers are usually available from industry sources or can be estimated from public financial data. General Product gets the following information about industry leader achievement:

General Products Benchmarking Outcomes

- Sales: Leader has 15 percent of market share for Product Y.

- Service: Industry best for customer service "Good+" ranking is 72 percent.

- Production: Production output per hour per employee is 21.

- HR: Industry leader's average employee turnover is 6.8 percent.

Now that the industry leader's achievements have been captured, you must determine your own achievement level in each area.

STEP 3 **Quantify your organization's current achievement in each business area.**

In this step you match the industry leader's achievements with your own in each business area.

General Product Current Achievement

- Sales: Market share for Product Y is 12 percent.

- Service: Customers rank our service as "Good+" 60 percent of the time.

- Production: Average production output per hour per employee is 20.

- HR: Employee turnover rate is 9.2 percent.

STEP 4 **Subtract your achievement from the industry leader's.**

This vital next step is relatively simple but often ignored. It is necessary to quantify the business gaps between the industry leader's achievements and your organization's current levels of achievement. The bottom line here is the quantity of performance you need to close the gap and achieve business goals for each team (in our example, sales, service, production and HR).

Determining the Performance Gap

Area	Current Desired Goal (Industry Leader)	Current Performance	Gap to Be Closed
Sales	15 percent	12 percent	Divisional goal to increase market share by 25 percent
Service	72 percent	60 percent	20 percent more "good+" ratings
Production	21 units	20 units	5 percent increase in output
HR	8.2 percent	6.2 percent	24 percent decrease in turnover

STEP 5 Determine the economic benefit of closing the business gap.

In this final step, you will determine the financial benefit of closing the gap. It may be beneficial at this point to enlist the help of someone with more experience evaluating financial value. While we give a brief overview of that process here, the information given is just that—an overview. The concept here is quite simple but the data is difficult to obtain and subject to controversy. Conceptually, you determine the business benefit of executing the strategy in dollars and the dollar cost of executing the strategy. This gives you the straightforward return on investment (ROI) formula:

[Benefits (in \$) – Expense (in \$)] / Expense (in \$) = The strategy value (as a percentage of the \$ invested expense)

This is the same type of calculation businesses make to decide whether to buy very expensive equipment, build a new factory, or issue debt instead of stock. The difficulty in making this calculation comes in determining the appropriate numbers for benefits and costs. For example, if General Products improves its product quality and sales go up, is the increase in sales due to the quality improvement? What about the increase in the sales commissions and the new marketing campaign that also happened in the same time period? How do you allocate those benefits? In the real world, many things are changing all at once, and you can never be 100 percent certain of how to accurately attribute a given change. Chapter 7 describes the staged innovation evaluation design, which provides ROI data about performance improvement at a 98 percent accuracy rate. Phillips (1991, 1994, 1997) has written extensively on the most principled methods for making ROI assessments.

Another problem with costing human performance interventions is that, unlike physical capital investments, the actual costs may not be clear. For example, the most important cost to be considered is the value of people's time. A common approach is to calculate some hourly cost based on fully loaded salary and benefits cost, but that calculation does not take into account the financial gains lost if the person is not using that time profitably. Some (e.g., Levin and McEwan 2000) recommend including a "replacement cost." Levin and McEwan's very conservative approach requires that ROI include the cost of replacing the lost labor of the person involved in a performance improvement program (that is, doubling the loaded salary and benefit cost) even if no replacement was hired.

The calculation can become complex as benefits accrue and costs are expended over a number of years. The benefit stream and cost stream are probably not constant over a number of years, so you need to factor in variable amounts. You have to make assumptions about how long the benefits will last and how long costs will be incurred, as well as any up-front or termination costs. Finally, you must account for inflation. (Phillips provides in-depth explanations of these techniques.) Financial analysts in your organization should be able to provide a return on investment estimate of the cost savings associated with each goal (see page 24 for suggestions). For example, working through just one of the factors from above would work in the following way.

- **HR: A 24 percent decrease in turnover will result in an annual business benefit of $225,000 in additional profit** (assuming 500 employees, $60 thousand per employee in fully loaded salary costs, 25 percent of first year salary cost to hire and train a new employee). This savings comes as a result of reducing the recruiting and training expense of 15 people a year (500 employees x 3 percent net reduction in turnover = 15 people x $60,000 per year in fully loaded salary x 25 percent expense for recruiting and training expense = $225,000). Now to get this increase in retention, General Products will need to spend an additional $150,000 per year on some relatively small changes to the benefits plan. This strategy would have a return of 50 percent [(225,000–$150,000) / $150,000] which is a very good return and therefore a worthwhile project.

STEP 6 **Identify individual and team goals that, if achieved, will close each gap.**

Once it is determined that achievement of business goals will be cost-effective, they must be translated for everyone in the organization. In other words, divisional goals such as those in the example above must be accompanied by what have been called cascading goals for every work team and individual whose activities will influence the achievement of each division's contribution to the bottom-line business goals. Individual and team performance goals link the jobs performed by everyone in the organization to the business goals. Teams and individuals need to know what they must accomplish this week (and next) to hit the goal. For example, everyone who works with customers must have specific goals that will eventually increase a customer's ranking of the service they receive. The short-term goals must be tightly linked to actions that will measurably improve customer service. These types of goals usually extend well beyond sales and human resources divisions. Sales may take leadership in increasing market share, and human resources or customer service may lead the attack on employee turnover rates and improving customer reactions to service. Yet everyone in the organization whose performance might influence the outcome must have team or individual goals that reflect their part in achieving each business goal.

Management Support

In our experience, the top management of larger organizations is usually focused on setting and monitoring business goals. The problem in large organizations is that business goals are not effectively translated for divisions, work groups, and individuals. In smaller organizations, managers often take on a variety of jobs so the setting and communicating of clear goals tends to be lower on their list of priorities. Too many managers in every type of organization have the view that repeating a mantra such as "We have to be focused on building market share and increasing our profit margin" is enough of a business goal for anyone. In fact, under most conditions, this type of general, long term and abstract goal is not at all helpful (Bandura 1997; Locke and Latham 1990). The issue should be "How much additional market share and profit must we achieve this month?" and "What is my/your/our specific part/role in achieving that market share and profit increase today or this week?" Researchers have studied how to set and communicate effective performance goals for many years. Strategies developed in research have been developed and tested in practice. There is no need to "fly blind" or start from scratch. Research on effective goals and the qualities of managers who are most successful at motivating people to accept performance goals is very helpful in this regard. See the sidebar on page 30 for the result of studies by Locke and Latham (1990) and Bandura (1997) in this area.

A colleague who works for a large technology companies found a way around top management indifference to translating business goals for teams and divisions. He sold the idea to a new regional manager who faced serious performance challenges. The regional manager agreed to a systematic goal-setting exercise using the most recent research. With the help of a vendor, he set up a divisional team and individual performance goal system where achievement was quantified and documented. The effects were so dramatically positive that other regional managers got interested and wanted a piece of the action. The idea spread outwards then upwards. Now nearly all of an organization with very independent regional managers has adopted the system, and it is supported by the top management. Swimming upstream with an idea is much more difficult, but success will get positive attention even when logical arguments fail to persuade top management.

When the top levels of an organization support the routine setting, translating, and communicating of performance goals, almost any type of performance improvement is possible. This has been the case with companies such as Procter and Gamble, the Semiconductor group at Texas Instruments, Florida Power and Light, and Hewlett Packard Company. All have not only set goals, but have worked to translate them clearly into both performance objectives and strategies for achieving goals for everyone in their organization. Without clear and accurate business and performance goals, all attempts to improve performance have less chance of success than pulling the handle on a slot machine.

Proposals From Vendors

Each organization has its own method of identifying vendors and contracting for services. The cautions and suggestions here are therefore somewhat generic with guidance on how to adapt them to specific procurement systems. First, you should simply do your best to clearly describe what you want to accomplish. Emphasize the need to assess the performance results of the system you will install. Next, be cautious with vendors who claim that what you want is not available or will be very expensive to develop. Beware of those who attempt to sell you something other than what you are requesting. Make certain that you ask vendors to suggest solutions that are compatible with the best and most current psychological and organizational research on goal setting and performance at work. Some of our clients have hired consultants with solid research credentials to analyze bids and make recommendations.

Many vendors want to provide you with a comprehensive performance improvement system or to substitute goal systems with Management By Objective (MBO) or "competency-based" programs. Many organizational specialists take the view that these approaches do not solve the goal system problem. A significant number of vendors now emphasize competency-based systems in place of performance goal systems. The people who advocate these systems offer to analyze your operation and suggest a master list of the performance competencies that are necessary to ensure success. Some competency-based approaches are more adequate than others, so we recommend caution. Many offer to provide very general goals tied to industry and common roles or jobs. One example required that people be able to "manage profit and loss, control expenses, and set and manage financial goals." Who could disagree? Yet these general competencies are only the beginning and cannot serve as work goals for teams or individuals. The only worthwhile competency-based systems focus on performance goals that are directly tied to an organization's business goals as the result of gap analysis. If high-level and abstract competencies help you get support for the goals that drive performance, they are positive. If they replace concrete, specific, and timely goals with general, abstract, and politically correct goals, they may be both distracting and destructive. The competencies you need from people will change as business goals change. Thus while we are positive about the potential of well-designed competency-based systems, we limit our enthusiasm to those where effective processes are used to identify, communicate, and track competencies. When little or no attention is given to identification of the essential job tasks needed to support shifting organizational goals, then the resulting performance improvement program is likely to be ineffective.

Many consultants offer Management By Objectives (MBO) systems for goal setting. MBO was an early consciousness-raiser and helped people value work objectives. Yet many professionals have genuine reservations about the utility of MBO today (Bechtell 1996). Most MBO systems communicate a bottom line goal to everyone, with no control over how the goal might be achieved and no clear vertical or horizontal linkages.

Prospective vendors may advise you to extend the scope of work beyond goal systems to include employee feedback on goal progress, training for goal achievement, and incentives for successful performance. It is easy to support effective feedback, training, and incentive programs when they are part of a carefully designed and integrated performance system. These issues will be covered in later chapters where specific advice will be given on how to choose an approach that fits your needs.

The trick when setting goals for individuals and teams is to determine how much capacity each has to invest when they are working at a peak. Then ask how much capacity it will take to achieve a critical goal. Then apportion capacity to meet goal requirements and out of this activity will fall a ceiling number of key goals for everyone. If you are wrong, adjust accordingly. The trial-and-revise learning curve on this process tends to be short when you monitor your goal assignment decisions during performance reviews.

Conclusion

Every organization needs to develop and communicate clear business goals that are translated into concrete, challenging, and current individual and team performance goals. Everyone in the organization needs to know exactly what work goals they must accomplish to support the achievement of the organization's most important goals. The identification of individual and team goals is different for various industries and market conditions. If an organization lacks a specialist with solid experience at this task, it is best to look for outside vendors.

We have started by developing clear business goals that are translated so that everyone understands the performance they must achieve in order to do their part to achieve business goals. What is not yet known is the distance between the current performance levels of teams and individuals and the goals they must reach. The next stage of the process is therefore to analyze the "gaps" between current performance and the level of performance necessary to successfully reach all business goals. The next few chapters describe how to determine the cause of each gap, whether enough support is in place to close the gap, and what kind of support would be most cost-effective.

Additional Resources on Performance Research

Topic: *Goal Setting; Importance of Goals in Work Performance; Types of Goals and Management of Goal Systems.*

Anderson, John A., Lynne M. Reder, and Herbert A. Simon. 1997. Situative versus cognitive perspectives: Form versus substance. *Educational Researcher* 26, no. 1: 18-21.

Kaufman, Roger A. 2000. *MegaPlanning: Practical tools for organizational success.* Newberry Park, CA: Sage.

Locke, Edwin A., and Gary P. Latham. 1990. *A theory of goal setting and task performance.* Englewood Cliffs, NJ: Prentice-Hall.

Mager, Robert F. 1997. *Goal analysis: how to clarify your goals so you can actually achieve them.* 3d ed. Atlanta: The Center for Effective Performance, Inc.

Phillips, Jack J. 1991. *Handbook of training evaluation and measurement methods.* 3d ed. Houston: Gulf Publishing.

———. 1994. *Measuring return on investment.* Alexandria, VA: American Society for Training and Development.

———. 1997. *Return on investment in training and performance improvement programs.* Houston: Gulf-Publishing.

3

Diagnosing Performance Gaps: Knowledge, Motivation, and Organizational Causes

IN ORDER TO CLOSE PERFORMANCE GAPS and achieve business goals, we first have to identify the cause of the gap and, therefore, the type of performance improvement program required. Chapter 2 described a method of identifying business goals and determining how much change was required to achieve them. While that process is absolutely critical, it is impossible for any real change to occur without taking that information to the next level: diagnosing the human causes and identifying appropriate solutions. This chapter extends the process to individual and team gap analysis so that performance specialists can do just that. We have drawn on solid research on performance to design a system for analyzing gaps in a way that will support the selection of effective performance improvement programs. This chapter will also

41

introduce our strategies for identifying scientifically-tested active ingredients in the various types of performance solutions available to close the gaps (Clark and Estes 1998, 1999; Estes and Clark 1999). Any business gap, performance problem, or opportunity to increase performance can be analyzed and solved using the research-tested process described in this chapter.

Let's begin by describing what research on knowledge, motivation, and organizational factors shows is the way to analyze performance gaps. The intent of this chapter is to help you identify where problems with these factors cause the gaps between goals and current performance. First, we describe some research-based, yet manageable, methods for analyzing gaps by identifying the knowledge, motivation, and organizational barriers to their achievement. Information on the big three causes will be collected by interviewing groups and individuals, looking at work records, and observing work processes. The information gained at this stage can be used to decide whether additional support is needed and to identify the type of support required to achieve goals.

The more novel and complex a goal, the more extensive the performance support required for people to achieve it (Clark and Estes 1999). Albert Einstein often warned that "everything should be made as simple as possible, but not simpler." The type of support people need can only be determined after an analysis of what is required to close a specific gap and whether those required elements are readily available in the organization. If they are available, then you only need to draw on local resources. If they are not available, then you'll have to build or buy them.

Though human performance is complex, research can help focus our efforts on the factors that have the biggest impact on work goals. The analysis process must help you survey people, examine records, and observe work processes to determine what is necessary to achieve goals. At this stage, it is critical to collect people's perceptions about the barriers they face in attempting to close the gap and achieve their goals. Perceptions of reality control performance. Different people can have very different perceptions about problems and solutions even when they share the same work goals. Gap analysis brings these perceptions out. Many performance specialists and managers jump too quickly and impulsively to select a solution after a quick and inadequate analysis of gaps. Others get hung up on trendy performance tools or try to solve a problem using methods designed and appropriate for an entirely different class of problem. How often have you seen a "how-to" training solution created when the real issue was a "why to," where no one believed the task was important?

The analysis process must also capture important documentation and other data about the goal and the links between relevant work systems. Adequate analysis of the reasons why goals are not being met (or identifying opportunities to increase performance) requires the review of many kinds of work records and other performance data. In this chapter we focus primarily on focus groups, interview, and survey methods. We feel that employee's beliefs and perceptions are critical to diagnosing gaps, and focus groups, interviews, and surveys are the best ways to identify beliefs and perceptions. Yet a complete gap analysis requires a good deal of creative searching for work records that support or fail to support people's perceptions. All presumed causes must be validated. Many of these other data sources provide vital insights about the reason for gaps. For example, most human resources groups keep records of employee absences, illness, complaints, transfer requests, and line manager assessments of individual and team performance. Computer systems are often set up to make a record of a huge variety of transactions in linked networks, such as who is accessing which intranet links for what reason. Accounting departments keep records of income, expenditures, purchasing requests, and problems. Customer service phone systems often have software features that record call times, customer complaints or complements, supervisor reactions, and the extent to which employees follow a prescribed approach. Consider the use of all of these sources of data and others that might give you an insight about the causes of performance gaps.

The "Big Three" Causes of Performance Gaps

Three critical factors must be examined during the analysis process. Those three factors are:

- People's knowledge and skills;

- Their motivation to achieve the goal (particularly when compared with other work goals they must also achieve); and

- Organizational barriers such as a lack of necessary equipment and missing or inadequate work processes.

The purpose of the individual and team gap analysis is to identify whether all employees have adequate knowledge, motivation, and organizational support to achieve important work goals. All three of these factors must be in place and aligned with each other for successful goal achievement.

In order to understand why knowledge, motivation, and organizational factors are important in analyzing gaps, think of a "people as cars" metaphor. Knowledge is our engine and transmission system. Motivation is what energizes the system—fuel and the charge in our batteries. Organizational factors are the current road conditions that can make it easier or more difficult to get to your intended destination. All people in organizations participate in a number of separate but interacting systems—but the knowledge and motivation systems are the most vital facilitators or inhibitors of work performance. These internal systems must cooperate effectively to handle events that occur in the organizational environment. A focus on one of the systems or on the organizational environment alone will only capture part of the cause and, eventually, provide only part of the solution.

Knowledge and Skills

During gap analysis, it is necessary to determine whether people know *how* (and when, what, why, where, and who) to achieve their performance goals. Because people are often unaware of their own lack of knowledge and skills or reluctant to disclose weaknesses, ask for their views about the knowledge and skill deficits of other people. Be clear you are seeking general information and not asking them to name specific people. Ask if those people have done something similar to the knowledge or skill in question in the past couple of years. Ask if they could do it if they really had to do it. If it seems that some or all of the people in their area do not know how, or can't "figure it out on their own quickly," then the knowledge component of the gap is a problem that must be solved. If people have not achieved this goal or a similar goal in the recent past, they may need more knowledge to achieve the goal. Also, poor communication and withholding important information are very common sources of knowledge problems at work.

Motivation

Motivational causes of gaps are a bit more complex than knowledge and skill causes simply because fewer performance specialists are familiar with them. Even though a significant amount of motivation research is conducted in organizations rather than in laboratories, the results have not yet been adequately communicated to people in work settings. In general, motivation is the internal, psychological process that gets us going, keeps us moving, and helps us get jobs done (Pintrich and Schunk 1996). Motivation influences three very critical aspects of our work and private lives—first, choosing to work towards a goal; second, persisting at it until it is achieved; and third, how much mental effort we invest to get the job done.

Organizational Barriers

Whenever people tell you about organizational processes that do not work or about inadequate resource levels, classify their comments as organizational barriers. These problems, such as missing tools, inadequate facilities, or faulty processes or procedures, prevent or delay work. Often, when knowledge and motivation can be ruled out, some form of organizational barrier is the culprit. Rummler and Brache (1995) and Galbraith (1995) compellingly illustrate how many organizational problems can be traced to business and work processes that are out of alignment with the business strategy or organizational structure. Also, whenever you modify the knowledge level or the motivation level of an organization, you will find the need to adapt the work processes accordingly.

Individual and Team Gap Analysis

There are many options for surveying opinions and beliefs about gaps. If you have in-house specialists in this area, then work with them. They know much more about your organizational culture and the problem you face than an outsider. You can also find many external consultants who will assist you in this task.

As we'll discuss later, performance is largely governed by people's beliefs about themselves and their environment. To redirect performance to new goals or to improve performance, begin by learning the beliefs and perceptions of the people doing the work—the people on the front lines. What do they believe is blocking them or their team from reaching goals? What kind of support do they believe they need? This is the type of information that is crucial to uncovering the causes of performance gaps. Interviewers do not have to agree with all of the views people will express, but it is absolutely necessary to listen actively and neutrally. While listening, analyze whether people are saying that their performance gaps are due to a lack of knowledge and skills, insufficient motivation, some organizational barriers, or some combination of the three.

The biggest mistake during gap analysis occurs when performance consultants believe that, because they are specialists, they understand how others think and feel about performance goals and gaps. Experienced analysts know that the people involved in a work situation can often have very unexpected opinions about problems and solutions. A related misconception occurs when performance specialists believe that their own past experience with people enables them to predict what people will do in new situations. There is solid evidence that our memory for the cause and solution to past performance gaps is changed by what is called "hindsight bias" (see page 46 for a description of Hoffrage's research on hindsight).

Our overconfidence may be one of the biggest barriers to identifying causes of performance gaps. Performance improvement specialists need to resist overconfidence and practice listening openly and fully to stakeholders. Only then can we resist jumping to solutions based on preconceptions of the problem.

- **Active listening, interviews, focus groups, and surveys**: If you decide to handle the gap analysis yourself, you can simply meet with individuals and ask them open questions which do not prematurely suggest causes. This procedure is outlined later in this chapter. Individual interviews are best if there are only a few people involved. Individual interviews also are very useful to pretest organizational surveys or focus group sessions where you will have only one chance—such as with senior executives, over-committed experts, or external customers. These interviews allow you to test the questions, gauge the range of responses, and spot political hot spots with much lower risk.

● **Selecting members of focus groups and individuals to interview**: If there are many individuals or teams in question, arrange for one or more focus groups. For most purposes, it is adequate to select about five to seven people at the same level who share similar performance goals and ask them to meet for an hour. A good rule is to select one focus group member to represent about five to ten people working in similar contexts. If the number of people involved is less than forty, consider individual interviews with two to three individuals who have the reputation of being mature, experienced, insightful and candid. If the number of people involved is more than forty,

HINDSIGHT IS NOT 20/20

Researchers suggest a common defect in our judgment about what worked in the past when gaps were closed (Hoffrage et al. 2000). It seems that our judgment about the future is sometimes dramatically changed when we learn about the outcome of a past event. When what happened is different from what we expected, we actually "reconstruct" the past—changing our memory about our previous expectations so that they are consistent with what actually happened. We remember that we predicted it even though we might have been completely wrong.

Let's say we had doubts or were only mildly positive about the benefits of a program we were implementing to solve a performance problem. Then, later (sometimes much later) we hear that the problem was solved after we decided to apply the solution. Our memory will be altered so that, in the future, we'll remember that we actually had a much higher confidence that the solution would work. The reverse is also true. An initial very high confidence is altered later after failure so we remember that we were skeptical all along.

This same quirk of memory also occurs when you learn about someone else's experience. Let's say that you read an account of someone who had a performance problem and claimed to have solved it with training. You will tend to remember that you also would have made a similar decision, even if you had rejected training as a solution in a similar situation.

Since most large organizations have training units or people charged with providing training services, training is more easily available than other types of organizational support. In chapter 2 we argued that most evaluation of training programs uses invalid "smile tests" that are widely but incorrectly believed to indicate that training

go for a focus group. For focus groups, try to select people from different teams to get a representative sample of many teams, as long as the teams all share common goals. Try to avoid mixing people at different management levels in the same group; few people are inclined to give candid advice about problems or solutions if a person at a higher management level is listening. In planning both individual and focus group interviews about the cause of gaps, it is best to decide ahead of time how you will recognize knowledge, motivation, and organizational barriers.

Problems with Interviews and Focus Groups

Critics of interviews and focus groups raise three issues. First, some worry that the selection of the groups will not be representative of all the stakeholders. If you have the time, these problems can be solved by randomly selecting the focus group members and interview candidates. If you do not have the time or latitude for random selection (the usual case), get the most representative sample you can and triangulate

was successful (when it may have had no effect or actually have had a negative effect). And since many performance goals are achieved without any support (even though training might have been provided), it is reasonable that even skeptical managers would often adjust their memory to give training the credit when it may actually have had no impact.

It is likely that inappropriate use of training is one of the major reasons why research on corporate training suggests that it accounts for only a 10 percent return on investment. This is, of course, an average. A well-designed learning solution applied appropriately to a knowledge gap may have a very high rate of return, as will be seen later. The problem comes when inappropriate training, which will have a zero or negative return, drags down this average. Impulsive use of organizational change strategies may be a significant part of the reason why the National Academy of Sciences review indicated that more than half of the change projects are reversed within one year after they are begun. And while there are few large scale studies of motivational programs, there is solid evidence that, when a number of the most popular incentives are provided at the wrong time and for the wrong reasons, performance declines.

Gaps between employee performance and work goals are a natural and desirable consequence of managing performance using cascading goal systems (chapter 2). As people work to achieve a clear goal, many gaps will be gradually closed without any extraordinary support. Yet other goals will require support ranging from routine to highly novel and extensive redesign of work activities. To read more about the hindsight gap, check Azar (2000).

by using multiple investigation methods. Check the focus group results with a few judiciously selected interviews with unrepresented stakeholders, with trusted colleagues, with astute observers either inside or outside the organization, and with blunt, outspoken people. Does a consistent picture begin to emerge? Do not overlook checking work records or other organizational data for evidence. Observe the work if possible. Talk to colleagues in other organizations or the staff of professional organizations. Use the time you have to collect the best data you can get; even a little well-selected data is much better than just guessing what people really believe.

The second concern is that aggressive people will intimidate those who are more introspective, or that highly verbal people will dominate the airspace. If you know that some very aggressive or intimidating people are selected, interview them separately rather than place them in a group where their behavior might silence or anger other members. During the focus group, it is your responsibility to control any inappropriate behavior. Otherwise, you lose the value of any data you are trying to collect and destroy your organizational credibility.

The third concern is that people will not give their candid views about problems in interview and focus groups. What is the incentive to be candid, and what is the political risk involved? The evidence is that people in groups are inclined to be candid about problems provided that they trust they will not be made personally responsible for the information they provide. Thus it is critical that the moderator or interviewer be viewed as trustworthy and act ethically. At the outset of the session, set the ground rule that what is discussed in the room is not for later attribution (the familiar "Four Walls" rule). Tell people exactly how the information will be used, analyzed, and reported. Control the session. Keep your confidentiality promises.

A very practical guide to this and other key issues in focus groups can be found at the following web site: http://www.cchs.usyd.edu.au/arow/reader/rlewis.htm. We urge you to get more information about how to set up groups and interview questions before conducting gap analysis. There are many outside vendors who provide this service. When doing it yourself, consider reading Greenbaum's excellent, research-based text on the issues (1998). The full citation is available in the list of references at the end of the chapter and the book. The abbreviated example of a focus group at the end of the chapter provides examples of how to classify what people say in focus groups and individual interviews.

Asking questions about the cause of performance gaps requires a great deal of advance planning. The goal is to classify the gaps described by participants into one of three categories—knowledge and skills, motivation, and organizational barriers to achieving business goals.

Interviews and Focus Groups: Tips for Clear Communication

STEP 1   **Conduct initial gap analysis interview.** Select a group of five to seven people for a focus group interview. You can select as many groups as you feel you need to get a good take on potential problems. You can also select individuals to interview alone. Interview people who have direct experience with the gaps and ask them to help you analyze the cause of each gap. Ask them questions and categorize each answer as an instance of knowledge, motivation, or organizational barriers causing the gap. Gaps may have more than one cause. Here are some examples of probing questions:

Open Question: What are the factors that are preventing us from achieving X goal? What do you see as the possible barriers to our achievement of X work goal?

Listen Actively: As people discuss their answer to your question, do not agree or disagree. Only check to make certain that you understand vague or confusing points by saying something like: "Let me see if I understand the point you are making" (then very briefly paraphrase what you thought they said), and ask "Is that it? Did I understand?" If they say no, ask them to rephrase their point. Your reactions must be neutral. *Do not agree or disagree, simply focus on understanding and recording their points.*

Knowledge/Skill Causes: Identify any point as a "Knowledge/Skill Issue" if someone suggests that people do not know **how** to achieve the goal or any aspect of the goal. Follow up with more specific knowledge/skill questions, as described in step 2.

Motivation Causes: Identify any point as a "Motivation Issue" if someone suggests that people will avoid, disagree, delay, refuse, and/or find excuses not to work on the goal. Follow up with more specific motivation questions, as described in step 2.

Organizational Causes: If people mention process and procedure issues or plant, equipment, and materials problems, then identify the comment as an "Organizational Issue." Follow up with more specific organizational questions, as described in step 2.

STEP 2 **Ask for more detail on each barrier issue suggested.** Some experts suggest letting people respond to the open question about barriers until they run down before following up with more specific questions. Others suggest asking specific, follow-up questions immediately after an issue is raised the first time to focus attention on the validity of the issues. Whichever of these two strategies you adopt, for each problem raised in response to the open question, follow up by asking more focused questions like the ones below.

KNOWLEDGE ISSUES:

Communication: Is the work goal clearly understood by everyone in your area? Was it communicated clearly?

Procedure: Do they all know *exactly how* to close the gap and achieve all parts of the desired goal? What parts of the goal do they not know how to achieve?

Experience: Have they ever accomplished a similar type or level of work in the past? If yes, describe the similar work.

MOTIVATION ISSUES:

Commitment: Are people persisting and spending enough time working to achieve this goal? Are they easily distracted from this goal by other, less important goals? Are they supportive of the goal in conversations? If the answer to any of these questions is no, you may have a commitment problem. Ask the following questions to determine the cause and record "no" answers:

- Do most people seem to expect a personal or team benefit from achieving the goal?

- If they do not like working on the goal, do they at least value the benefits of having achieved it?

- Is there any negative consequence if they do not achieve the goal? Do they understand the risk of not achieving the goal?

- Is their mood toward the goal positive or neutral? (If many people are angry or depressed about the goal, answer this question with a "no.")

Under-confidence: Are people making mistakes and worried that they are not able to achieve the goal? Do they think that they will be prevented from achieving the goal? If the answer to any of these questions is yes, under-confidence may be one of the problems you must solve.

Overconfidence: Are people making mistakes but taking no responsibility for them? Are they blaming others or the system for their mistakes? Are people using the wrong strategies to achieve goals but not recognizing their errors? Are they avoiding or rejecting corrective feedback about their mistakes? A positive answer to any of these questions may indicate an overconfidence problem.

ORGANIZATIONAL ISSUES:

Take each performance gap and ask people who are familiar with the problem if the following descriptions accurately represent the people who are working in the area where the problem exists. Record negative answers because they indicate a possible Organizational Barrier problem.

Tools: Do they have the necessary tools, materials, and work space to achieve the goal?

Process: Do business processes effectively and efficiently support the goal?

Procedures: Are established work procedures adequate to support the goal?

STEP 3 Write a brief summary of your conclusions: Summarize the results of the interviews you conducted. Use the headings Knowledge Problems, Motivation Problems, and Organizational Barrier Problems. If it is clearer to subdivide the three causes further (Motivation into Commitment Problems, Under-confidence Problems, and Overconfidence Problems, for example), go ahead. Under each heading, describe the evidence you found for and against the contribution of each factor to the achievement of the goal. Validate the causes that seem to be important by looking at work records and other documentation. Conduct follow-up interviews if necessary. Document your summarizing conclusion about the cause(s) of each gap and the evidence that leads you to your conclusion.

Example Focus Group Session

The following dialogue is "creative reconstruction" of a focus group from an actual performance improvement case recounted by Jim Fuller in *Performance Interventions* (1999).

Jim the Performance Consultant Hi. Thanks for coming here today. As you know, meeting the financial goals for our division calls for a 15 percent increase in sales. While we're doing a good job of increasing sales to existing customers, the only way to get the level of growth we need in our market is to gain new customer accounts. Experience shows that we need a strong advertising campaign in place in a given territory before it makes sense to call on new prospects, yet these advertising campaigns are not being launched. Our goal today is to shed some light on the reasons why we are not advertising to attract new customers in our territories. As sales reps, who have responsibility for all selling activities in your territories, including advertising, you're in the best position to know. What are the reasons why we're not advertising anywhere near enough? Let's focus first on reasons and possible barriers to advertising and not get into solutions at this point.

Tom	Well, there are probably all kinds of reasons. There certainly isn't enough time in the day to do all the millions of things that need to be done.
Jim	So time for advertising is an issue? (*As Tom nods, Jim writes "too little time-motivation" on a flip chart.*) Thanks, what else might be a factor?
Brenda	Well, I think Tom just about nailed it with time. We're swamped now making calls, and there's just no time for do advertising, especially in a bureaucracy like this!
Jim	(*reflecting and paraphrasing*) Sounds like it's pretty frustrating to be asked to do advertising with so little time and bureaucratic hurdles in your way. (*As Brenda nods, Jim adds to his list on the flip chart "bureaucratic policies."*) What kinds of red tape procedures get in the way?
Brenda	Well, for starters, any expense over $500 needs a gazillion approval forms filled out and you have to get your boss, your boss's boss, and the bean counters to sign off before they'll cut a check. (*The nods and noises of agreement show that Brenda has hit a nerve, and Jim notes "burdensome expense approval process."*) Most of the time, if I do any advertising, I end up putting it on my own credit card and waiting around to get it back. At least I get the bonus airline miles from the credit card company. (*Group laughs and claps, and Jim notes "disincentive—$$$ from own pocket up-front."*)
Jim	Thanks, Brenda. Other ideas?
Carl	Maybe this isn't politically correct, but writing jingles and slogans just isn't my job. I sell office equipment.
Jim	So writing advertising is outside the scope of your job? (*Jim writes down "Not a sales responsibility? Clear roles?"*)
Martha	Carl, you know that isn't so. You just don't like doing it. And I don't like it much either. But I do it. Sometimes. (*Jim is writing "Motivation."*)
Raul	One big reason we don't like it is because we don't know how to do it. I've never had any training in writing advertising. Anybody here had any training on this? (*Heads shake, and a chorus of "no" is heard.*) How are we supposed to do it without any training?
Jim	Thanks. (*Jim writes "Don't know how to write advertising."*) What else?
Patti	Hey, Raul, where are we supposed to get the time to go to this training? Didn't we start this whole thing off by saying we just don't have enough time? After all, a dollar is a dollar.
Jim	I'm not sure I understood all of that.

Patti   What part of too little time did you not understand?

Jim   (*laughing*) I got that part, but what did you mean by a 'dollar is a dollar'?

Patti   We're sales people. We carry a quota, and we get paid a commission based on what percentage of that quota we achieve. Sales volume. Period. End of story. Filling out forms doesn't count. Sitting in a training class doesn't count. Writing advertising doesn't count. And if I'm in the Top Ten Club selling to my existing accounts, why would I waste time knocking on new doors where they've never heard of us?

Jim   So you're saying that selling to existing customers is easier than selling to new accounts and counts the same toward quota? (*Jim adds "incentives for new accounts" to the list.*)

The conversation continued, and Jim continued to elicit new ideas, listen reflectively and check for clarification, and make preliminary notes about root causes. When the focus group was completed, he gathered his notes, analyzed the results, and found the following:

- Almost all the sales reps were achieving quota by selling to existing accounts. Since there was no special incentive to sell to new accounts and those sales required extra work, they were not making the effort.

- The sales representatives did not know how to conduct a good advertising campaign, as they had no training and background. In addition to not knowing how to write the ads, they did not know what made a good ad, where to place the ad, how to get it placed, how frequently to run it, or any of the other basic skills of advertising.

- Any ad campaign was going to cost more than $500, and the approval process for expenses was cumbersome and deeply resented.

Jim analyzed these root causes as follows:

- Reps were meeting quotas without selling to new customers and did not need to do the advertising work to be successful. They did not like writing advertising nor did they have any incentive to do it. In fact, working on the advertising was punishing for them as they had to run around getting signatures and often put up their own money up front. Since they were achieving quota there were no negative consequences for them. How can the incentive system be modified to build commitment?

- Not knowing how to conduct an advertising campaign is clearly a knowledge issue. At first, it appeared that maybe there was some confusion about roles and responsibilities with Carl's comment, but further discussion clarified that they really didn't know how to do it or where to start and that they really had never successfully accomplished similar tasks. So there is a knowledge gap, but is there too much to learn about advertising? Is the gap too big to close with training in the time available?

- The expense approval procedure is clearly getting in the way of desired performance. How can the goals of these controls be met without interfering with developing advertising?

All of these causes would have to be validated using the types of resources we described earlier. A fuller version of the gap analysis process is illustrated in the case studies at the end of the book. This example, however, does show how all of the big three causes of performance problems are interrelated in complex problems, and how techniques such as focus groups can help separate them out. Clearly, the solution set designed for this problem area will need to address each identified cause. No matter whether you design and create an intervention yourself or purchase one, the intervention must have specifically targeted active ingredients in order to work. Rossett (1999, 1987) provides an excellent resource for a fuller discussion of the gap analysis techniques summarized here.

Conclusion

The next three chapters explore each of these root causes in depth: knowledge and skills, motivation, and organizational barriers. Each chapter will indicate the specific active ingredients needed to attack the root cause. Select a combination of the active ingredients that solve the problem and can be adapted for your people and organization. This list becomes the basis for either your design document or your product evaluation criteria, depending on whether you are making or buying a performance solution.

Additional Resources on Performance Research

Topic: *Analysis of Performance Gaps; Management of Human Performance Projects*

Azar, Beth. 2000. Blinded by hindsight. *Monitor on Psychology* (May): 28-29.

Ericsson, K. Anders, and Herbert Alexander Simon. 1999. *Protocol analysis: Verbal reports as data.* Revised ed. Cambridge: MIT Press.

Fuller, Jim. 1997. *Managing performance improvement projects: Preparing, planning, implementing.* San Francisco: Jossey Bass.

Fuller, Jim, and Jeanne Farrington. 1999. *From training to performance improvement: Navigating the transition.* San Francisco: Jossey-Bass.

Greenbaum, Thomas L. 1998. *The handbook for focus group research.* Beverly Hills: Sage.

Mager, Robert F., and Peter Pipe. 1997. *Analyzing performance problems: or you really oughta wanna.* 3d ed. Atlanta: The Center for Effective Performance, Inc.

Rossett, Allison. 1999. *First things fast.* San Francisco: Jossey-Bass/Pfeiffer Publications.

Rummler, Geary, and Alan Brache. 1995. *Improving performance: Managing the white space in organizations.* 2d ed. San Francisco: Jossey-Bass.

Stolovitch, Harold D., and Erica J. Keeps, eds. 1999. *Handbook of human performance technology: Improving individual and organizational performance worldwide.* 2d ed. San Francisco: Jossey-Bass.

4

KEY POINTS
➤ Types of Knowledge and Skill Enhancement
➤ The Active Ingredients: Recent Developments in Knowledge and Skill Research
➤ Knowledge and Skills Solution Requirements
➤ Debunking Knowledge and Skill Myths

Knowledge and Skill Gaps: Information, Job Aids, Training, and Education

THIS CHAPTER DESCRIBES RESEARCH-TESTED APPROACHES to closing performance gaps that are caused by a lack of knowledge and/or skill. This chapter summarizes some recent developments in research on knowledge and skills and their application at work, on how we learn complex knowledge and skills, and on the role of knowledge in the development of advanced professional expertise. It then suggests the minimum requirements for cost-effective information, training, and educational programs to support the achievement of performance and business goals. At the end of the chapter we have included a checklist to rate the compliance of training courses or workshops with the recent developments in knowledge and skill research.

Types of Knowledge and Skill Enhancement

Knowledge and skill enhancement are required for job performance under only two conditions. First, they are required when people do not know how to accomplish their performance goals, and second, when you anticipate that future challenges will require novel problem solving. The first condition usually indicates a need for information, job aids, or training. The second condition suggests a need for continuing and advanced education. There is often confusion about the differences between these four terms, so we will begin by defining them.

Information

When we tell people something about their jobs they need to know to succeed on their own, we are giving them *information*. If people do not need help practicing in order to apply the information successfully, then information is all that is necessary to reduce their uncertainty about how to achieve a performance goal. The simplest type of job information we give people is to suggest that, for example, they "handle this sales challenge the way you handled the one two months ago." It helps people identify strategies or procedures learned in the past that can be helpful in particular situations.

Job aids

A slightly higher level of information is in the form of *job aids* that contain self-help information employees can use on the job to perform a task. Job aids provide people with recipes for achieving performance goals in a form that permits them to do it on their own. Job aids are a form of information that is most cost-effective when people do not require guided practice to achieve a complex performance goal. Job aids can be provided to people who have completed training and need reminders about how to implement what they have learned. They are also very useful for experts who are being asked to use a new approach but do not need training. For example, a job aid that summarizes the actions and decisions that must be made to implement a preferred sales approach for a new product line might support the transfer of training for novices—or serve as the only performance support received by experienced salespeople.

Training

Training is defined as any situation where people must acquire "how to" knowledge and skills, and need practice and corrective feedback to help them achieve specific work goals. Another way to think about training is that it is information (and sometimes job aids) *plus* guided practice and corrective feedback. Training can result in high impact learning in any context—in a classroom or office, on the job, off the job, on the Internet or Intranet, or at home. Since a growing number of trainers are claiming that only "on the job" training is effective, it is important to stress that this view is not supported by research (see for example, an excellent discussion on the topic of "situated learning research" by Anderson et al. 1996, 1997). Training is not defined by its setting, although the job context of the examples and practice strategies one uses in training can have a considerable impact on its results. For example, when teaching a desired sales plan to employees who are not very experienced in sales, training would provide all of the how-to strategies, opportunities for guided practice, and expert feedback required to learn the new scheme.

Education

Education is any situation in which people acquire "conceptual, theoretical, and strategic" knowledge and skills that might help them handle novel and unexpected future challenges and problems. Education should not be expected to provide "how to" information since we cannot anticipate ahead what needs to be done on the job in highly novel situations. Education is current research-based knowledge about why things happen and what causes things to happen. Education can also happen anywhere—in a university, on the Internet or the Intranet, at home, and on the job. Like training, the impact of education does not necessarily depend on the setting where it takes place. For example, an education that would support the development of future sales strategies to help a business negotiate unexpected future changes in a market might require that a person get an advanced degree to master basic principles in psychology, economics, sociology, business, law, or engineering.

The Active Ingredients:
Recent Developments in Knowledge and Skill Research

The following eight points highlight some of the most recent developments in knowledge and skill research. These developments should be used as guidelines for selecting effective performance improvement products. Using the checklist at the end of the chapter will ensure that a program complies with these developments.

REALITY 1

Information, job aids, training, and education provide different benefits and should be used in different circumstances.

We have already gone over the definitions in brief of the four ways of developing knowledge and skills, but here is some more extensive information about the situations in which to use each type.

Give information or job aids when experience or bare procedures will manage familiar or routine tasks. Information and job aids are the least expensive form of knowledge/skill development. These two kinds of support are useful in two different levels of a familiar situation. Let's say that people seem not to know how to achieve a performance goal. Have they achieved a similar goal in the past? If so, they only need the *information* that they should apply the approach they used in the past (or a slight variation) to this new challenge. People often have problems recognizing when it is appropriate to use past experience to handle a new challenge. Psychological researchers call this a "knowledge transfer" problem. Past experience is stored in our long-term memory along with information on its conditions of use. For many people, the conditions of use statements we learn are too specific and restrictive, and

---

INADEQUATE INFORMATION, JOB AIDS, TRAINING, OR EDUCATION CAN MAKE PERFORMANCE WORSE.

Debunking the Myths

Many people believe that when instruction fails, nothing happens. The perception is that a failed effort to provide knowledge and skills results in a lost opportunity, but the trainee ends up more or less where they started. This is a curious belief since failure in nearly all occupations can cause serious harm. Consider the consequences of serious mistakes by physicians, pharmacists, lawyers, airline maintenance technicians, and CEOs. Patients are harmed when physicians make mistakes. People are harmed by legal malpractice, planes crash as a result of human error, and companies fail when CEOs blunder. Why should training mistakes have no consequences?

In fact, training can have serious negative results. Some types of training may actually damage some trainees' future use of knowledge and skills. As discussed in chapter 1, inadequate or inappropriate training can result in trainees who perform worse after training than they did before it began (Clark 1989). These situations are not well documented in research because of the tendency of scientists not to report studies where the results were the opposite of what was expected.

Most of the evidence points to two primary kinds of damage. First, poorly organized training information can disorganize previously learned knowledge about any set of topics. This often happens when too much or too little structure and control are imposed on training information or on the rules for navigating during training. The resulting mental disorder makes it difficult or impossible later to remember and use facts, concepts, and the way that processes operate in the topic area of the training. This condition also prevents the use of subtle but important interconnections between the types of knowledge we had about the topic prior to beginning instruction. These conditions are classified as "knowing less" since less knowledge can be effectively used after training than before. The research test for this effect is a significantly higher pretest than post-test knowledge score.

they need help recognizing that the challenge they face is similar to one they mastered in the past.

Another possibility is that the content they need to know is simple to assimilate. Perhaps there are two well-known and plausible approaches, and to keep people working together, you want them to use "A" and not "B." If you communicate clearly, just telling them may be enough. Generally speaking, regardless of the level of performance intervention you select, you will need to communicate information clearly as a necessary component of your solution set.

When information is not enough, a *job aid* that contains the essential "how to do it" information (often in brief, checklist form) is adequate support for most people to achieve many performance goals. Job aids are the best alternative when people

The other type of damage occurs when inadequate or wrong job information is presented during instruction and results in trainees learning incorrect knowledge and skills. These strategies are then used at work by people who believe they should work and who overconfidently reject feedback to the contrary. This type of experience can often be seen at work, when something "everyone knows" turns out not to be so. Christman (1999) reports the case of a major avionics manufacturer falling further and further behind on essential training for their aircraft, despite a large training development group. Christman suspected that the group had learned faulty and divergent processes, although he was continually assured that "everyone knew" the official process. Upon closer examination, it turned out that no two people in the group of thirty shared the same model, and many of their fundamental assumptions were not only wrong but conflicting.

Another example of this effect is when trainers provide wrong analogies or metaphors for critical knowledge or skills being learned. For example, kids who learn that the structure of atoms is like the structure of the solar system (the nucleus is like the sun and the planets that circle the sun are like the electrons circling the nucleus) have been found to have difficulty learning chemistry (Clark 1989) because the analogy is wrong (electrons of like charge repel each other, but planets attract each other). People who are told that thermostats work like the accelerator in a car (the higher the setting, the more "heat") often waste large amounts of energy. They try to heat their offices or homes by setting the thermostat at a very high temperature because the analogy implies that the house will heat faster if the setting is higher. By the time they realize the house is too hot, they have wasted energy. Norman (1988), one of the founders of cognitive science, discusses many examples of these misconceptions in his excellent book *The Psychology of Everyday Things*. Gilovich's *How We Know What Isn't So* (1991) discusses how learned misunderstanding of basic statistics leads many people to make serious errors in life and business. These are only a few of many knowledge consequences of inadequate instruction.

need to perform a new procedure in a job area in which they already have a lot of experience, or for important tasks that are rarely encountered. One familiar example of rare but important tasks are safety procedures such as using a fire extinguisher or exiting a building in case of a fire. Job aids are preferable when people do not need guided practice and expert feedback in order to successfully master a new approach. Job aids have to be carefully designed and tested in trial-and-revise cycles to ensure they are complete and accurate. Wrong job aids can do more harm than good. Yet if they are adequately designed, job aids can greatly reduce the cost of acquiring new knowledge and skills.

Use training when employees need demonstration, guided practice, and feedback to perfect a new procedure. When learning to accomplish job tasks requires a higher level of knowledge and skill support than job aids, *training* is often required. Training is necessary when the goal faced is just new enough that people will not benefit from a checklist job aid of "what to do" or a procedural job aid that describes "how to do it." In order for training to be cost-effective, you have to ensure that people do not know how and are not able to benefit from information or job aids alone. They require the next higher level of knowledge and skill support: training involving guided practice applying new knowledge and skills and corrective feedback during their practice. Training can be provided in any context, provided that instructors can observe trainees and give corrective feedback during the early part of practicing a new skill. Training does not have to happen in a classroom or even at work. Computer and web-based training can be just as effective as classroom or on-the-job experience, provided that it is designed to support learning and performance, and application examples and practice exercises are focused on job application.

Provide education for novel and unanticipated problems. The primary benefit of information, job aids, and training is to support the learning of how-to knowledge so employees can achieve recurring, known job tasks. However, people cannot be trained in advance to accomplish job tasks or solve job-related problems that are unexpected, novel, and non-recurring. How would you begin to prepare people for the unexpected?

The only way to equip people to handle the novel and unexpected is with *education*. A good education provides people with solid but general conceptual and analytical knowledge. This knowledge is often in the form of new and important concepts (new terms or variables), vital processes (descriptions of how things work), and current theories or principles (research-based theories about cause and effect) (Anderson and Lebiere 1998; Anderson 1993; Barsalou 1992). The best advanced degree or certificate programs also offer new ways to understand how to use the knowledge gained in education to solve novel problems. A number of businesses have collaborative arrangements with solid "professional" Masters and Doctoral level programs in areas such as business, education, engineering, organizational or performance psychology, organizational design, economics, and law in top universities. These are the best educational investment for business. In addition, our own research suggests that one of the most powerful ways to prepare employees to make use of an education is to teach them to summarize and translate research for the development of new and powerful human performance "technologies" (Clark and Estes 1998, 1999; Estes and Clark 1999). This also can be seen when business recruits people with research training in the physical sciences and mathematics to develop new technology products, cutting edge software, or complex new financial instruments such as derivatives.

Educating people provides organizations with the capacity to generate new conceptual knowledge that will solve novel problems and handle novel job challenges when they occur. Obviously, education is a long-term business investment, whereas information, job aids, and training have a more immediate and tangible payoff. Yet when do you anticipate a novel and unexpected challenge to your business? This week? This month? This year? Can we afford not to make the longer-term educational investment in an organization that plans to be healthy next year, let alone a decade from now?

Figure 4.1

Knowledge And Skill Problem Solution

Four types of knowledge and skill solutions and when to use each type:

1. Not using relevant past experience that will achieve goals? **Information**

2. Not enough relevant past experience but related expertise? **Job Aids**

3. No experience or related expertise but routine procedure? **Training**

4. Not prepared to anticipate or solve a novel future challenge? **Education**

When your analysis indicates that knowledge and skills are required to close a performance gap, you must determine the solution that will close the gap. Check to see what kind of knowledge and skill problem has been reported and verified. Is it that people need to do something now that they've done before? If so, make plans to give them that information in a form that gets their attention and incentives to use the information on the job (see chapter 5 for a discussion of work motivation). Are they experts at what they do but they need to do something new in their area of expertise? Plan to provide that information and a job aid that describes the new procedure they must use to achieve their work goals. Check to see if they need any training to implement the job aid. If they have a limited knowledge and skill background but need to learn a new approach or procedure for tackling job tasks, make a plan to give them that information, job aids that summarize the new job procedures, and training that pulls it all together with an opportunity to practice and get corrective and supportive feedback. Finally, if the gap that needs to be closed has to do with preparedness to solve novel problems as business conditions change, education is the solution.

Corporate Universities

The recent enthusiasm for corporate universities may be due in large part to frustrations with the perceived benefits of the formal educational programs offered by independent colleges and universities. Most corporate universities appear to have been formed by renaming and consolidating existing training groups and related personnel functions. Nearly all corporate universities are actually providing training.

The movement toward corporate universities may be an opportunity for organizations to begin implementing the science-based, analytical, business goal-oriented approach described in this book. Many, but not all, training managers and performance experts support the movement away from training departments to corporate universities. Recently a number of critics of the training function have suggested that if the function identifies its mission as training, the temptation is to treat all performance problems as knowledge and skill problems and "solve" them with training. Corporate universities can help overcome this limitation by enlarging the role of training specialists. In the corporate university, the emphasis can be widened to include analyzing the cause and solutions for performance gaps and providing access to services to close these gaps in cost-effective ways. Corporate universities can develop partnerships with certified, degree-granting universities or research and development centers and other performance service providers. They can become the repository and proactive organizer and manager of the knowledge and skills the organization develops over time. By the definition we have outlined earlier, these corporate universities are long-term investments. Motorola, Royal Dutch Shell, and GE receive a lot of media attention for various levels of attempts to incorporate some of these new gap analysis and closing features into their corporate universities.

REALITY 2

In training, structure and sequence job knowledge as the job is performed.

Training influences how we organize our professional knowledge. If the information coming in is disorganized, it is much more likely that our mental connections having to do with that knowledge will also be disorganized. The level of mental organization and the links between new and familiar knowledge have a major impact on how much we can remember and use the knowledge in solving problems.

In training, knowledge must be outlined and structured so that it is presented in the same sequence that it is used or applied on the job (Anderson and Larabie 1998; Tobias and Fletcher 2000). The first step in accomplishing a job goal should be the first thing trainees learn, the second thing they do should be learned second, and so on. When there is no necessary sequence to the parts of a job, it is best to present simpler knowledge before information that is more difficult and complex. This sequencing should dictate the outline of all training courses. While it seems simple enough, it is a radical departure from the way that information is sequenced and presented in most training courses.

Most training specialists assume that knowledge is best presented in the same way they experienced it in school. Teachers usually begin with historical, theoretical, and conceptual knowledge about topics, and then, if there is time, some practical application. The practical application, if it is ever presented, is usually not very practical at all. In defense of teachers and schools, how could anyone know in what context a student will apply knowledge and skills? How would you teach how-to knowledge and skills to 30–35 students, all of whom may end up in completely different vocations? Application knowledge must be very specific in order to have value for most people at work. Except for what are called "tool subjects" such as mathematics, reading, and communication, the how-to knowledge taught in schools must be very general. Even tool subject knowledge is taught with generic examples that may not help people apply what they learn at work. This is why most people in business complain that high school and college graduates do not know how to *do* much of anything.

Also important in the decision about structuring job knowledge and skills for people is strong and counterintuitive evidence that most of what we learn is bound to context. We might learn a lot of mathematics in school, but not be able to use it to compute the financial consequences of different types of mortgages or to manage our personal finances. An example of this phenomenon can be found in a well-known research study of shoppers. People who had demonstrated their ability to transform fractions to make accurate cost comparisons while grocery shopping were unable to make the same type of computations when asked to solve non-shopping fraction problems as part of a research study (Chi, Glaser, and Farr 1988).

REALITY 3

Experts who train are sometimes wrong, so use trial-and-revise cycles.

Recent developments in research on the nature of advanced work expertise has yielded a number of surprising results. One focus of this research is to describe the types of knowledge that experts use to complete tasks and solve problems. Recent findings estimate that between *50 and 90 percent* of expert knowledge and skills are automated and unconscious (Bargh and Chartrand 1999; Clark and Estes 1999, 2000; Kirsch and Lynn 1999; Glaser et al. 1985). This unconscious knowledge is both a great strength and a well-disguised weakness. The strength is that unconscious knowledge allows the expert to perform very complex tasks quickly, effortlessly, and accurately, and to think about other issues while working. The weakness is that because the knowledge behind routine but complex tasks is unconscious, experts cannot accurately describe how they perform those tasks. Almost all work-related training is designed and/or delivered by subject-matter experts (SMEs). If SMEs are trying to describe to trainees their expert approach to solving work problems, and their expert approach is automated and unconscious, then the SME will inevitably make mistakes or fail to relay pertinent information which can cause learning problems for trainees (Dienes and Perner 1999; Ericsson and Simon 1999; Bereiter and Scardamalia 1993).

To illustrate unconscious knowledge, think about the expertise you possess that aids your identification of different types of animals. How do we so quickly identify a cat and know that it is different from a very similar mammal such as a dog or an opossum? If you had to describe the difference between cats and dogs to a child, what exactly would you say and do? The knowledge you use to classify them is automated. Another example is to think about how you learned to drive a car. Initially the process was difficult and stressful, but now you drive almost without thinking about it (until something unexpected happens), because your driving expertise is automated and can be applied unconsciously (while you listen to the radio or talk to a companion). If you have ever tried to teach someone to drive a car, you know that you must continually correct your explanations because your "trainee" cannot do what you have just described to them. Some trainers are tempted to blame the trainee, when in fact, it is often their own poor quality explanation that may contribute to learning and transfer failures.

The experts who serve as training designers and presenters most often do so without understanding the nature of their own knowledge and skills, how learning occurs, or what type of training support aids job performance. Most of the expert-trainers employ what some have called the "spray and pray" approach to instruction and learning, meaning that they spray their audience with a lot of information and pray that they are able to learn and apply it. The problem with this approach is that a significant amount of the information experts provide in training has critical gaps and errors, precisely because so much of their performance is informed by unconscious knowledge (Bargh and Chartrand 1999; Clark and Estes 1999, 2000; Glaser 1990; Glaser et al. 1985). They unintentionally give out wrong information or fail to give enough information. What makes the problem even more difficult to solve is that, in general, experts believe that their descriptions are complete and accurate. The gaps and inaccurate procedures trainees receive from experts must be corrected later at work. The correction process is a drag on performance for some trainees and a performance stopper for others. This phenomenon is a key factor contributing to poor return on investment from training. An investment in correcting this major fault in our training systems can produce an extraordinary return. So how can this problem be prevented?

Beta Test Trial-and-Revise Cycles: In smaller training exercises or when you have a small number of trainees, the preferred approach is to make certain all training designed and/or delivered by an expert is subject to a systematic trial-and-revise cycle before being implemented fully. This process adds some time and expense to the training cycle, but it is also likely to increase the return on investment by huge amounts. It requires only that you insist on a Beta test with a small group of trainees similar to the larger group who will receive the course to be presented. The results of the Beta test should be used to adjust the accuracy of the training until Beta trainees can perform the tasks accurately.

Cognitive Task Analysis (CTA): When you need a larger training course, use cognitive task analysis (Clark and Estes 1996; Schraagen et al. 2000) to provide accurate knowledge. CTA provides a highly accurate description of how a top expert performs a job for the purpose of training others to do the same thing. The approach allows the extraction of how-to information from experts in interviews. This information can then be embedded in training. With a combination of observation, interview, and testing experts' advice, CTA provides compelling evidence of the many mistakes experts make as they tell novices how they solve problems. Cognitive task analysis was developed in the military and medicine to extract highly complex knowledge from advanced experts. In its early stages, it was used to determine how top design engineers found and corrected errors in complex avionic systems for fighter aircraft or how doctors diagnosed complex diseases. Researchers have estimated that with CTA, it is possible to capture job knowledge that takes experts about five years to develop in about fifty hours of information for use in training. CTA will be the foundation of the next generation of knowledge and skill management systems in support of complex work performance.

REALITY 4

Training objectives should be clear and linked to performance and business goals.

All training courses, lessons, and discussions must begin with a clear and concrete description of what the trainees will learn and be able to do when they finish the exercise. Trainees need to know what performance goals they will be able to accomplish as a result of the training. This seems to be an obvious and simple-minded suggestion, but it is very often ignored in training courses. When it is ignored, trainees substitute their own goals for the course—and their goals may not support

---

KNOWLEDGE AND SKILLS ENHANCEMENT INCREASES PRODUCTIVITY MORE THAN INCREASED HOURS OR CAPITAL STOCK INVESTMENT.

While poor training and education can make things worse, effective knowledge and skill enhancement has a better investment impact than increasing work hours or acquiring capital stock. In the early 90s the National Employers Survey studied about three thousand employers and found that, even in manufacturing, increases of about 10 percent in appropriate training, capital stock, and work hours produced corresponding productivity increases of 11 percent, 6.3 percent, and 3.9 percent, respectively. (EQW 1995). In service and other non-manufacturing industries, the impact of education was even higher. This is evidence for the saying that there is more benefit from "working smarter, not longer."

Work-related knowledge and new skills are not ends in themselves for any business. Nor does everyone necessarily have a right to or a need for training or education at work. Over time, however, it is an essential means to achieve business goals in any organization. New knowledge and skills are required when work undergoes rapid and sustained change. Increases in both the quantity and quality of change in business require changes in our knowledge about work. The recent computer and Internet revolution at work is only one example of a major knowledge and skill challenge for workers.

The irony revealed in U.S. studies is that training seems to be mainly targeted at management and not widely distributed throughout organizations. Only about 20 percent of workers say that they get any training from their employers, and those who do are largely in managerial jobs or are college-educated workers. *Training* magazine's annual study of training in organizations continually reports that while

their eventual job performance. What happens most frequently is that course writers or expert trainers give trainees a vague introduction, such as "This course is about Java Script" or "I'm going to describe the new accounting system." In fact, the actual objectives of the two courses are: "You will learn to write Java Script so that you can develop new shopping Bots for our system" or "You will learn to identify and correct accounting mistakes." Clear and specific objectives focus people's attention on their eventual job performance. They enhance both learning and the transfer of knowledge and skills to the job after training.

One way to establish clear objectives is to summarize the key points to be delivered in training and put them up front so that people can be thinking about them (Corkill et al. 1988). These are called advance organizers by researchers because they help people efficiently organize the knowledge they receive during training. Advance organizers are a very inexpensive way to help people structure the knowledge they

approximately 70 percent of the organizations that reply to their survey train middle and upper managers, only about a third to a half train production and service employees. It is important to note that the *Training* sample is voluntary and not a representative sample, so is probably skewed toward organizations that favor training. The fact that others studies show only about one in five employees getting any training suggests that a more accurate picture is even more dismal than the one reported by *Training*.

Existing studies make very few distinctions between the very different conditions that surround training and educational decisions. What are the benefits of knowledge and skill investments in workers who need to learn new ways to achieve business goals? Asking the question in this way would probably show results that would far exceed the 11 percent increase in productivity found with a 10 percent increase in worker education. Actual productivity gains and return on investment may end up being much higher with targeted training and well-planned educational experiences.

There are good examples of high ROI from training and education programs targeted to business goals. For instance, Christman's intervention (page 61) resulted in a 3000 percent ROI in just the first year (1999). Boyd (1999), another contributor to *Performance Interventions*, details how a process redesign coupled with process-specific training had an ROI of 120 percent and an inventory reduction of $10 million for a consumer goods company. Reel (1999) presents the case of a telecommunications company whose process redesign and training resulted in a $14 million reduction in injury expense for an ROI in excess of 1000 percent, as well as the considerable goodwill from corporate responsibility. There are relatively few studies, but where they occur, they tend to find dramatic results from specific, targeted investments.

receive in ways that will make it easier for them to transfer new skills to their job. Disorganized knowledge is one of the major barriers to its seamless application in practical settings. How many times have you had the "I knew that" experience as someone else suggests an approach to a problem that you knew about but did not think to use or suggest? These transfer failures are very common. People often know how to solve a problem or accomplish a work goal, but they do not remember relevant past experience. Another source of disorganized knowledge is in the lack of structure we build into job information and training. The less structure imposed on incoming information, the more disorganized the resulting knowledge.

Many of the principles covered here are consistent with the basics of instructional design and the standard ISD (Instructional Systems Design) covered by Dick, Carey, and Carey (2001), for example, and the very effective approach to instructional design clearly described by Mager (1997). The ISD model works well for training that presents relatively simple knowledge and has served corporate training well within that scope. The need for workers to learn more complex knowledge and accommodate newer approaches to learning has pushed the limits of traditional ISD (Van Merrienboer, Clark, and de Croock n.d.). Designing instruction for complex knowledge requires more cognitive approaches, such as the one created by Van Merrienboer (1997). Merrill's Five Star system (2001) provides promising techniques for evaluating these newer design models and methodologies.

REALITY 5

Avoid high interactivity, exploration, and other learner control training strategies.

Many trainers are attracted to so-called "discovery," "exploratory," and "learner control" instructional strategies in computer and web-based training. The essence of these approaches is a computer-based or on-line training course in which the trainee is encouraged to learn by exploring the information available. Dazzling sound and graphics and highly flexible navigation possibilities are the current epitome of too many technology-based training experiences. The basis for these training and educational methods is a controversial ideology called radical constructivism. Radical constructivists begin from the premise that people construct their own knowledge by forming and linking concepts in unique and individual patterns, which is an accepted tenet of mainstream cognitive theory. The radical constructivists, however, go further. They make the untested assertion that people cannot benefit from instruction that directs them to perform in a certain way, and instead, each person must develop his or her own unique procedure for each skill (Anderson et al. 1996, 1997). This controversial and unsubstantiated idea, if true, would imply that each of us must essentially reinvent all wheels as most instruction is, in principle, fruitless, if not outright destructive. Solid research indicates that while discovery, learner control, and high levels of interactivity might help a small percentage of the most advanced experts, they are not helpful for 95 percent of the people who need training or education (Clark 1988; Cronbach 1966; Sweller 1994).

In discovery or learner control methods, trainees might start at the end of a course or lesson and drift around, sampling whatever appeals to them. They may or may not look at important information, take a test, or practice any of the knowledge and skills being taught—depending on their interest level. The alarming aspect of this trend to use navigation in training courses is that there has been powerful evidence for more than thirty years that these strategies not only do not help achieve specific job goals, they can cause harm (Cronbach 1966).

The result of the discovery approach is that trainees may like their training experience, but the job knowledge they acquire is largely disorganized and inadequate for application. Even trainees who want to learn will be distracted and defeated by these well-intended but destructive training methods. Most damaging is that trainees do not notice that their knowledge is disorganized and ineffective in helping them achieve job goals.

While flexible navigation through large bodies of information is not a desirable feature for training, it might be very beneficial for *educational* goals. The best educational experiences can sometimes be enhanced by allowing our interest to determine which problems we think about and solve. Creative insight sometimes happens when we allow our minds and attention to wander. Training, however, must be focused on performance and business goals.

REALITY 6

Training must show trainees exactly HOW to decide and act to achieve performance goals.

This suggestion is the heart and soul of all training. Effective training must provide, in each lesson or segment, a specific procedure that shows trainees exactly how to accomplish a performance goal. The procedure must be described completely and clearly. It must describe how and when to make all necessary decisions and follow up with all necessary actions on the job. These procedures need to be sequenced as performed on the job and must be accompanied by demonstrations of the procedure, by opportunities to practice them during and after training, and with feedback to correct performance mistakes.

Most training courses only tell trainees what to do, and not how to do it. These two types of information are very different in appearance and impact. For example, telling someone to solve a problem is very different from telling them exactly how to solve the problem. The first is "what to do" information, and it helps people use what they have learned in the past. But if they have not learned how to do something in the past, information on what to do is less than helpful. When people do not have relevant experience, they need clear, accurate, job-related "how to do it" training.

As discussed in relation to expert trainers, one very important fact to understand about human knowledge and skills is that much of what we know is unconscious. There is evidence that most routine job knowledge is also automated and unconscious, and so new knowledge and skills must be learned in such a way that, when it is appropriate, it will be edited until it is accurate and then automated. Yet many training specialists are largely unaware of the importance of automated procedural knowledge in job performance. Ninety percent of training emphasizes only 10 percent of the knowledge we need to learn. A special issue of the American Psychologist in June of 1999 was devoted to research on this kind of knowledge. In that issue it was suggested that approximately 90 percent of all of our knowledge is automated and unconscious.

TRAINED AND EDUCATED WORKERS DO NOT QUIT TO GET BETTER JOBS ELSEWHERE.

Debunking the Myths A major factor in the resistance to providing expensive education or training for employees is the concern that they will leave and take the investment with them to a new company. Yet all evidence to date suggests that this fear is groundless. Some people do choose to change their jobs. Yet an increase in personal marketability because of training and education does not seem to be an important factor in the decision to move.

In fact, there is evidence that under some conditions, investment in knowledge and skills enhancement can actually increase employee retention and reduce replacement costs. A groundbreaking study by Louise Parker (1993) found strong evidence that people who feel effective at work and believe that they have interesting development opportunities tend to stay with an employer. Adequate training and individual development plans would therefore contribute to employee retention. In exit interviews, departing employees most often cite "increased salary and benefits" as their reason for taking a new job. Upon closer inspection, Parker found that this is seldom the reason that people change employment, although it may be a more acceptable excuse for leaving, in addition to closing off potentially embarrassing questions during exit interviews. It appears that most people are more inclined to leave an employer when they feel that they can no longer be reasonably effective in their jobs and/or continue to develop into new responsibilities.

If the "they'll get trained and move" fear is well founded, then more people would change jobs during or after times when training investment is highest. Conversely,

The remaining conscious 10 percent may be critical, but it should not dominate training at work.

One of the great research success stories in the past two decades is the amount and importance of what has been learned about knowledge and how it functions in job performance. Yet the lag between the conclusion of field research on new approaches and the communication of important findings is still intolerably long. For example, very critical work on different knowledge types was more or less completed in the 1970s, and the results are only now being disseminated widely. Most state-of-the-art knowledge and skills systems for organizations are or will be built around the insights that have come out of this work.

Because of severe limitations on how much we can think about at one time, our mind automates all knowledge that we use repeatedly. In this way, we can think about new challenges, rather than wasting precious thinking space for challenges we have already mastered. Once we automate knowledge about any task, we tend to forget the conscious knowledge because we no longer need it. Psychologists agree

fewer people should switch jobs when training investment is low. In fact, according to a number of national and regional studies, this has not happened. *Training* magazine's annual study of the investment in training by business organizations is a key factor in our argument. In the early 90s, investment in training was the lowest in the decade (and even lower than in the previous few years) because of consolidations and job cutting (*Training* 1992). A 1991 AMA study indicated that over 50 percent of the companies surveyed said that they had cut jobs and workers (AMA 1997). Yet in 1992 and 1993 the number of people who reported preferring to remain in the same job regardless of the amount of training and education they received remained remarkably stable. In fact, the number of employees who say that they prefer to remain with their current employer has remained at about 60 percent for the past two decades (Bond, Galinsky, and Swanberg 1998).

This stability continues even when distinguishing between top performing employees and those at middle or lower levels. Managers often suggest that job commitment is higher for less skilled workers because they have fewer options. If this is true, then the most technologically savvy workers might be the most risky targets for education and training investment. Yet *Wired* magazine's national study in 1997 indicated that about 70 percent of the most technologically savvy workers were committed to their employers, as compared to a marginally higher commitment rate of 80 percent for those at the lowest levels of technological knowledge and skills (Katz 1997). The factors promoting retention go far beyond training. There is ample evidence to refute the claim that investments in employee training lead to employee turnover.

we can only think about only a very small number of things at one time. Estimates range from a high of nine to as few as three items. Yet even with nine items in our conscious mind at one time, how would we manage even simple work tasks? Remember those jokes about people who can't walk and chew gum at the same time? If all knowledge were conscious, this would be a true statement for all of us.

Any knowledge we are aware of thinking is, by definition, conceptual. It is made up of all of all of the facts, concepts, processes, and principles we are aware of having learned and can remember and think about. The automated, unconscious facts, concepts, processes, and principles is the "stuff" of educational experiences. Its purpose is to help us handle novelty. Automated knowledge can be "muscular" (how to do tasks with our hands or bodies) and "decision-based" (how to solve problems and make complex decisions). This is why advanced experts are so quick and accurate when solving complex problems—they have a huge store of automated expertise. This is the type of knowledge that we use most often at work. Most knowledge starts out as conscious and conceptual but gradually changes form with use and becomes unconscious. Training people effectively requires giving them accurate procedures, practice, and corrective feedback that permits them to gradually automate the knowledge.

REALITY 7

Ensure that knowledge and skills learned in training and education transfer to the job.

What is learned in training is usually applied on the job, right? The research literature on training and education is full of examples of failures to transfer learning back to the job. Many experienced trainers believe that less than half of what is learned in training actually transfers back to the job. The research on this topic suggests that a more realistic estimate is much less than half (Stolovitch 1997; Ford and Weissbein 1997). Since we seldom evaluate transfer back to the job, it is important that investments in training be protected by paving the way for transfer to occur. What prevents transfer and what enhances it?

The major factor influencing transfer is the attitude and actions of the managers and supervisors of people who are trained. The success rate is much higher when managers prepare employees for training beforehand, letting them know that whatever they learn in training should subsequently be applied back on the job. In addition, successful managers ensure that people are practicing their new skills within seventy-two hours of finishing the training, monitor performance, and coach (or provide coaching for) people who are having difficulties. The biggest barrier to transfer (other than failures to provide useful learning during training) is a "forget that stuff, we do it my way" attitude on the part of supervisors or negative attitudes from coworkers. The more that managers enable people to learn and use their new knowledge and skills, the greater the level of transfer achieved. The more that managers support the immediate application of knowledge and skills and provide monitoring and coaching, the more enthusiastically people apply what they have learned.

REALITY 8

Integrate solutions.

Remember that the results of gap analysis most often indicates a need for a mix of information, job aids, training, and education. This mix must be designed, developed, and implemented to close the gap. We recommend, however, waiting to design or implement knowledge and skill solutions until these programs can be fully integrated with motivational and organizational process and material changes (chapters 5 and 6). Wait for implementation until you have finished the complete analysis of motivational and organizational solutions to gaps and stretch goals. Fully integrated performance improvement programs are more effective, much more efficient (Fuller and Farrington 1999), and considerably easier to evaluate.

CHECKLIST: KNOWLEDGE AND SKILLS SOLUTION REQUIREMENTS

1. Knowledge and skills you intend to provide are structured in the most efficient way by using the following model:

   - If they have accomplished a very similar goal in the past, provide "do it again" Information.   _____

   - If they have experience in related job area(s), provide "how to do it" Information and Job Aids.   _____

   - If they will perform this task a number of times, provide Information, Job Aids, Training with practice and feedback.

   - If they must be able to handle unexpected problems, provide Education about all possible problem areas.   _____

2. The information, job aid, or training sequences the different job tasks and goals *as they are performed* on the job. If there is no necessary sequence, simpler learning goals are tackled before more difficult goals. _____

3. Drafts of information, job aids, and training will go through trial-and-revise cycles (using cognitive task analysis or trials with representative groups) to make certain that all information is accurate and clear.   _____

4. All of the information, job aids, and training provide clear learning objectives that are linked to performance objectives and business goals.   _____

5. Advance organizers and learning, performance, and business goals are placed at the beginning of all information and all segments of training presentations.   _____

6. Job aids and training have been designed to focus trainees on exactly how to decide and act so that performance goals will be accomplished.   _____

7. The training requires all trainees to practice the skills they're learning in the same way they would apply the skills at work to achieve performance goals.   _____

8. Coaches or managers will monitor trainee performance and give both positive and corrective feedback when necessary to help them identify their strengths, correct misunderstandings, and apply their knowledge and skills on the job.   _____

9. Managers will prepare all trainees to use the knowledge and skills they get from training by meeting with them in advance. Trainees will be required to use the information they get in training within 72 hours after finishing.   _____

Additional Resources on Performance Research

Topic: Knowledge and Skills; Information, Job Aids, Training and Education; Knowledge Management

Anderson, John R., and Christian Labiere. 1998. *The atomic components of thought*. Hillsdale, NJ: Lawrence Erlbaum Associates.

Anderson, John R., Lynne M. Reder, and Herbert A. Simon. 1997. Situative versus cognitive perspectives: Form versus substance. *Educational Researcher* 26, no. 1: 18-21.

Bargh, John A., and Tanya L. Chartrand. 1999. The unbearable automaticity of being. *American Psychologist* 54, no. 7: 462-479.

Bereiter, Carl, and Marlene Scardamalia. 1993. *Surpassing ourselves: An inquiry into the nature and implications of expertise*. Chicago: Open Court.

Bransford, John D., Ann L. Brown, and Rodney R. Cocking, eds. 1999. *How people learn: Brain, mind, experience, and school*. Washington, D.C.: National Academy Press.

Clark, Richard E. 1988. When teaching kills learning: Research on mathemathantics. In *Learning and instruction: European research in an international context*, edited by H. Mandl, E. DeCorte, N. Bennett, and H. F. Friedrich. Vol. 2.2. Oxford: Pergamon.

Cronbach, Lee J. 1966. The logic of experiments on discovery. In *Learning by discovery: A critical appraisal*, edited by L. S. Shulman and E. R. Keisler. Chicago: Rand McNally.

Dienes, Zoltan, and Josef Perner. 1999. A theory of implicit and explicit knowledge. *Behavioral and Brain Sciences* 22, no.5: 735-755.

Druckman, Daniel, and Robert Bjork, eds. 1994. *Learning, remembering, and believing: Enhancing human performance*. Washington, D.C.: National Academy Press.

———. 1991. *In the mind's eye: Enhancing human performance*. Washington, D.C.: National Academy Press.

Resnick, Lauren B. 1987. *Education and learning to think*. Washington, D.C.:

Schraagen, Jan Maarten, Susan F. Chipman, and Valerie L. Shalin. 2000. *Cognitive task analysis*. Mahwah, NJ: Lawrence Erlbaum Associates.

Sweller, J. 1994. Cognitive load theory, learning difficulty, and instructional design. *Learning and Instruction* 4: 295-312.

Tobias, Sigmund, and J. D. Fletcher, eds. 2000. *Training and retraining: A handbook for business, industry, government, and the military*. New York: Macmillan Reference.

Van Merrienboer, Jeroen J. G. 1997. *Training complex cognitive skills: A four-component instructional design model for technical training*. Englewood Cliffs, NJ: Educational Technology Publications.

5

Motivation Gaps: Belief Is (Almost) Everything

WHAT WOULD IT BE WORTH TO YOUR ORGANIZATION if 40 percent of your employees enthusiastically worked the equivalent of one extra day each week for no extra pay? Though that may sound unattainable, this level of increased performance can be achieved by eliminating unnecessary "demotivators" and replacing them with positive motivational support focused on closing performance gaps. Spitzer (1995) reports that half of all American workers confess that they invest only the minimum effort required to avoid being fired. A whopping 84 percent admit that they could work much harder at their jobs. Let's assume that less than half of those 84 percent might work only 20 percent harder if they were more motivated. How much value would that amount of extra effort add to the bottom line in your company? What would it cost to achieve this added performance? Motivation is an area where tangible benefits are available to organizations even when there is no gap between goals and current performance. This chapter identifies some of the most important active ingredients in successful motivational products and services to help you select research-tested strategies for increasing performance motivation. It also describes tested methods for solving motivation problems, some common practices that reduce or destroy motivation, and ethical and effective strategies to lead people to work harder.

Many organizations base their motivational systems on outdated, wrong, or incomplete strategies (Spitzer 1995). Few of us would allow a surgeon to operate on us if their knowledge of brain structures was twenty years out of date. Ask yourself how much it would cost to implement some of the research-based suggestions in this chapter about how to increase work motivation—and what the return might be on your investment.

What Is Motivation?

Human beings are made up of two very distinct yet cooperating psychological systems—knowledge and motivation. Knowledge tells us how to do things and is our storehouse of experience. Motivation gets us going, keeps us moving, and tells us how much effort to spend on work tasks. Experienced, intelligent people who are unmotivated lack the direction, persistence, and energy to accomplish much at work.

Active Choice, Persistence, and Mental Effort

Most motivation researchers agree that there are three motivational "indexes," or types of motivational processes that come into play in a work environment. These opportunities or potential problem areas are:

1. when people *choose* (or fail to choose) to actively pursue a work goal;

2. when people have many goals and distractions and so are tempted not to *persist* at a specific goal—we allow ourselves to be distracted by less important goals; and

3. when people have chosen a goal and are persisting at it in the face of distractions, but have to decide how much *mental effort* to invest in achieving the goal.

Active Choice: Someone has made a choice when he or she begins to pursue a goal actively. Even if they did not select the goal themselves, when they are actively working towards it (as opposed to procrastinating, avoiding, arguing, or delaying), they can be considered to have chosen that goal. The intention to do something is not an example of choice; only active pursuit of a goal counts.

Persistence: Few people have the luxury of a single work goal. Once a person has chosen and begun working on a goal, they usually have to divide their attention between many other goals. When people get distracted too often or for too long by less important (but perhaps more attractive) work goals, they have a persistence problem. In general, it is desirable to have the greatest amount of persistence invested in the most important work goals.

Mental Effort: Finally, choosing and persisting must be accompanied by adequate mental effort invested in key work goals. If a goal is routine and people can draw on past experience to reach the goal, it may not require much mental effort. Novel or unanticipated challenges require a great deal of mental effort to succeed. Mental effort is determined, in large measure, by our confidence. Those who lack confidence tend not to invest much mental effort in a task. Why should people work hard when they believe they will fail? *Under-confidence* often leads to persistence and choice problems.

People also invest little mental effort when they are *overconfident*—when they have misjudged their own abilities. An overconfident person thinks that he knows what he is doing and that the task is a no-brainer, so he does not work very hard to complete it. Confidence is good, but overconfidence can cause people who make mistakes to take no responsibility for them. People who are challenged by the task but are neither overconfident nor under-confident seem to invest the most mental effort. Figure 5.1 illustrates the three facets of motivated performance.

Figure 5.1

Three Facets of Motivated Performance

| **Active Choice** | **Persistence** | **Mental Effort** |
| Intention to pursue goal is replaced by action. | Once started, we continue in the face of distractions. | People work smarter and develop novel solutions. |

Increased Performance
Increased motivation combines with effective knowledge, skills, and work processes to result in goal achievement.

© 2002 CEP Press

Fostering Mega-Motivation: Beliefs and Effectiveness

The first and perhaps most important thing to know about motivation at work is that it results from our experiences and beliefs about ourselves, our coworkers, and our prospects for being effective. Beliefs result from our interpretations of past experiences and are not always accurate. In fact, many psychologists now generally believe that people are better off if their beliefs about themselves are somewhat more optimistic than is warranted by objective and realistic assessments of their capabilities. While extreme overconfidence can be destructive, mild overconfidence can be very beneficial. People who are pessimistic or believe that they cannot be effective no matter what they do will not actively pursue work goals, persist so that they avoid distractions, or invest enough mental effort to do their best. They tend to become depressed or angry when they hit routine barriers. Other things being equal, people who are positive and believe that they are capable and effective will achieve significantly more than those who are just as capable but tend to doubt their own abilities (Bandura 1977, 1997).

To illustrate just how powerful beliefs can be, take the example of the effect of placebo medications. Approximately one in six Americans is taking (or has taken) medication for depression. Yet, the premiere American research journal, *Science*, reported in 1999 that 75 percent of the effectiveness of all antidepressant medications subjected to clinical trials are due not to the medication per se, but instead to the placebo effect. When people believe that a pill is going to make them better, they very often get better even though they are taking an inert sugar pill that does not contain the active ingredient in the antidepressant medication.

There have been many theories about what causes human motivation. In the past, some researchers have attributed motivation to reinforcement and the contingencies placed on behavior at work. Others emphasized the need to balance pleasure and pain, the dominance of survival instincts, or the need for self-actualization. Still others point to the need for personal independence and freedom at work. These different points of view have caused many arguments in the research community and elsewhere, some so active that researchers complain that competition between motivational research groups is actually discouraging future motivation studies!

More recently, a number of researchers have studied all these points of view in an effort to synthesize the different views into one powerful and inclusive approach. Those meta-studies have centered on one primary human motive that seems to drive all or most of our motivated activity (see Hardt and Rodin 1999; Ford 1992; and Klein et al. 1999). Psychologists call this root motive by a number of names: "expectancy and control," "efficacy and agency," and "effectance." For the purposes of this discussion, we will call it "effectiveness." The emerging consensus finds that the root motive influencing all human behavior is a *desire to be effective* in our lives. Our motivation for work is therefore controlled by whether we believe the environment provides us with work goals and resources that can result in a reasonable amount of effectiveness. People tend to measure all choices in each context against a personal "effectiveness measuring stick." We choose, persist, and expend mental effort only on those activities that appear to have the most impact. The difference between us is that different people have very different ideas about what makes them effective.

Cultural and Personal Differences in Effectiveness Beliefs

If all people are motivated by effectiveness needs and expectations, then why isn't it easier to foster work motivation? Why are there so many different motivational programs and strategies out there? The essential reason is this: while everyone is motivated by the drive to be effective, there are cultural and personal differences influencing people's beliefs about what makes them effective. These differences sometimes produce diametrically opposed motivational styles for different groups, so that what motivates one person or group might be neutral, or even negative, for another.

Some of our consultant colleagues were working with a manufacturing client with equivalent plants in the US and Central America. Faced with the goal of reducing costs without lowering salary or sacrificing equipment, the American divisional VP adopted the goal of lowering the large employee turnover (about 35 percent in some jobs). Part of her program involved giving line workers more control over how they did their jobs to increase their persistence. This "empowerment" strategy has been used successfully in many American organizations. Presumably, giving people more control over how they do their jobs increases their feelings of personal effectiveness and therefore their incentive to stay with an employer. Since turnover was tracked on a weekly basis, the team managing this program had good baseline data to begin the program.

The program started producing a solid increase in retention in the United States almost immediately. However, there was no change in the foreign operations. When the team investigated, they were told that the program had been stopped almost as soon as it was announced because workers had rejected it and threatened to quit. In focus groups, workers in the Central American plant reported that they would not be able to meet production targets if they were deciding on work processes. They asked instead for "stronger managers" and "clear direction."

After analyzing the two situations, the performance improvement team concluded that the workers in the two plants had very different ideas about what made them more effective. The more independent personal and work styles of people in the

American plants led them to decide on their own work processes enthusiastically. In the other country, however, personal and team effectiveness was viewed as a function of the influence of supervisors and managers. This view was validated in a short study where focus groups of assembly workers were asked to rank the "influence" of line supervisors. Those supervisors who were judged to be "stronger" had significantly less employee turnover in their areas. While it is not valid to make generalizations about different countries' cultural or work ethics from this example, this experience does illustrate a crucial point: different individuals and groups can have very different beliefs about what makes them effective. We can never assume that our beliefs will automatically be shared by those around us.

Cultural effects operate constantly but quietly within our multinational organizations. Currently researchers are examining the cultural, regional, and individual differences in people's beliefs about the different ways they can achieve "effectiveness." The existing research on this topic has already identified a number of such culturally-based motivational differences, including "I" versus "We" beliefs, mastery versus performance motivation, fixed versus flexible ability beliefs, and internal versus external control beliefs. The next section will briefly describe two of these differences: "I" and "We" cultures, and internal and external control. Chapter 6 discusses culture at work in more depth.

"I" and "We" Cultures

Group- and team-oriented "We" cultures do not necessarily value personal initiative above other qualities or search out situations where they have more autonomy. They tend to view themselves as an integral part of family, social, and work groups more than as separate individuals. They tend to be cooperative and invest maximum effort in group settings when the group determines that a goal is important. "We" cultures value collective efforts, and individuals working independently are viewed as isolated and sometimes even as pathetic (Winter 1996). "We" culture individuals tend to value teamwork and may often work harder in collective efforts than "I" culture people. A colleague explained the "We" culture outlook by explaining that he was raised "to think of myself as a finger on a hand—not as the hand or the intelligence directing it. 'What is the worth of one finger on one hand?'" he asked. "The strength and benefit of a hand is in the smooth cooperation between the fingers, not in the independence or competition between fingers."

People from "I" cultures tend to work hard as individuals and prize independence when they personally accept the value of a work goal. Many "I" culture people think of collective efforts as less interesting, and they tend to loaf more in group settings unless their individual contributions to the group are assessed. They tend to work harder and are more committed when they have more influence over their jobs and when they are consulted about matters that directly influence them. It is easy to see how motivational programs promoting autonomy and individual initiative or promoting teamwork and collaboration could run up against conflicting cultural styles.

Internal and External Control Belief Cultures

One of the most studied of all cultural and individual differences focuses on beliefs about the causes of important events in our lives. Some cultures and individuals hold the more internal belief—that they are individually responsible for much of what happens to them and that their skill has a direct and important influence on their lives. Internals do believe that external forces influence their lives, but they believe they can only directly control their own efforts and so focus on their individual contribution to events in order to achieve their goals. Internals are the product of "I" cultures and families.

More external people tend to believe that the important events in their lives are not caused by anything they have done or failed to do, but instead by external forces. While externals do accept that they can have an impact on personal events (they often try to influence events indirectly), they believe that most of the important things that happen are not under their direct control. External people are more often the products of "We" cultures and families.

All of us are internal in some contexts and external in others. Many Westerners tend to be highly internal at work but somewhat more external in their religious beliefs. As you might imagine, these two belief styles produce very different motivational dynamics. Work internals may make a stronger commitment to work goals where they believe that their skills will be tested and individual competition is encouraged. They may invest greater mental effort when convinced that their personal expertise will grow if they master a difficult task. Work externals, on the other hand, might more easily commit to performance goals where they believe that the outcome cannot be easily predicted and where luck might play a big role in results.

Avoiding Stereotypes and Handling Conflicting Cultural Beliefs

Wide variation in individual and group styles exists within every culture. It is wrong to assume that because a person grew up in a certain culture that they will necessarily possess the values associated with their origin culture. However, it is crucial to recognize the different cultural values that exist at work and ask people to tell us what makes them effective or ineffective. Any steps you take to analyze and close performance gaps must take these different cultural values into consideration. Performance improvement specialists and managers need to be prepared to accommodate what often seem to be diametrically opposed beliefs about which work conditions are optimal for motivated performance. How is it possible to tailor work so that it reflects opposing beliefs and values?

The issue of conflicting beliefs is handled every day by political and organizational leaders. The strategy most often used is to motivate people to accept visionary goals and social programs by calling on the full range of cultural values. For example, politicians routinely send the message to all of the "internals" in their audiences that success requires their individual participation, effort, advice, and skills. Almost in the same breath, they will tell their more "external" supporters that the outcome of the coming election will be determined by destiny, that they have a mandate to win, and that they can expect good fortune and will succeed.

The way to avoid cultural stereotypes and to overcome opposing beliefs is, first of all, to conduct a thorough gap analysis. Ask people to describe what they need to make them effective. Incorporate all of these suggestions into a motivational program. When managers or coaches describe the conditions and/or benefits of achieving work goals, they must incorporate apparently conflicting cultural and group values that turn up in interviews and focus groups. It is generally believed that people will select the motivational message that reflects their own orientation.

Barriers to Motivation

Cultural stereotypes and mishandling cultural differences are only a couple of the ways that people in organizations can discourage performance. The first barrier to motivating other people is our own motivational beliefs and attitudes, and some beliefs should be arrested for "motivational homicide." Many managers believe that motivation is inside a person and that it cannot be influenced much by any outside person or environmental event. With this view, you can categorize people's attitudes about work with labels that range from "lazy" to "passionate." You can assume that there is not much you can do to transform a person who is working only enough to keep a job into one who is passionate and driven to excel. This view is not only wrong, but it is one of the main barriers to fostering maximum work motivation.

Motivation is the product of an interaction between people and their work environment. Think back over your own work experience. All of us are more motivated at some times and in some contexts than at others. Most of us are more energized when working on some types of tasks or with certain types of people in specific settings. Nearly all of us have been energized by visionary people or great work environments.

Some managers believe that motivation is exercising control over people. They believe there is a magic combination of monetary rewards and threats of punishment that will cause people to do what they wish. This view grows out of the over-application of behavioral psychology. Excellent human performance in today's organizations is a complex phenomenon and grows out of passion, belief, expectation, and expertise. The relationship between monetary reward and motivation is not a simple, linear one. Monetary rewards and some research-based ideas on how to apply them are discussed later in this chapter.

Some motivation advice you will hear emphasizes what goes on in employees' heads. Yet it is not possible to directly control what goes on in people's minds. Other motivational strategies are targeted to the work environment. Intelligent and targeted changes to the work environment can indirectly influence motivation, but arbitrarily changing the environment does not ensure that people will be more motivated. To improve motivation, your goal must be to indirectly influence people's understanding of the impressions they create in others, about their own ability to do a job, and their beliefs about the personal or group benefits of work.

Elements of Work Environments That Destroy Work Motivation

There are five elements of work environments that most researchers agree are the main destroyers of motivation.

1. **Vague and constantly changing performance goals and feedback:** In the absence of clear business and performance goals, people substitute their own goals, which may not support the bottom line. Vagueness and inconsistency in a work environment lead most people to assume that anything goes. Without clear goals and feedback, people are not committed to work and are not inclined to target business goals with their best efforts (Locke and Latham 1990).

2. **Dishonesty, hypocrisy, and unfairness:** Managers often feel that they must tell innocent lies or change their minds about promises made earlier in a weak moment. Sometimes they make quick and arbitrary decisions out of frustration with difficult people. Most of us do not believe that when we do these things we are lying or being hypocritical or unfair. Alternatively, sometimes policies and practices managers strongly believe in are reversed or changed by senior management. Old practices and agreements may become suicidal due to changing market realities. In either event, something communicated and promised to people must change. People at work are all adults, right? This is the way the world works, so get over it! Yet our opinions about our own behavior are much less important than how our behavior is perceived by those around us.

   Perceptions control personal motivation, not reality. And when people perceive those around them as unfair, dishonest, or hypocritical, the best one can hope for is that they will act mature, ignore those conditions, and work hard despite it all. Yet even the most mature people are not going to work as hard when they experience dishonest and unfair behavior. It is more typical that organizational dishonesty and unfairness are viewed as an invitation to respond in the same manner. Remember, trust is difficult to gain and easy to lose. Trust is a major factor in work motivation and de-motivation. When supervisors or managers are perceived as unfair, hypocritical, or dishonest, trust is lost. Once lost, trust is difficult but not impossible to regain. Keep in mind that people's perceptions of honesty and fairness are the motivational issue (Bandura 1997).

3. **Unnecessary rules and work barriers:** Many people point to the huge variety of arbitrary and seemingly unnecessary rules and cumbersome policies as one of the major demotivators at work. Even the most competent and personally motivated people tend to quit trying in the face of what they perceive to be arbitrary barriers. Is it really necessary to formally request accounting approval for all purchases more than $50? Consider whether the form is actually preventing a problem or causing a bigger problem because of people's resistance to filling in forms. What is gained by rules that people can't talk or eat in certain areas? Are you absolutely certain that dress codes are necessary and that they add value to your business? How much of people's behavior must you control to achieve business goals?

   Some organizations generate so many rules that they are mutually contradictory. Even rules that might be good, intelligent policy, when combined with too many others, may produce contradictions and unintended side-effects. Organizations with too many rules become bureaucratic, leading to situations where violating some rule is unavoidable. These catch-22's lead to intense frustration, anger, and cynicism, and are damaging psychologically to individuals and groups. A rule-heavy situation may even lead to anarchical behavior, with people assuming that even the fundamental values and standards of business conduct are just "red tape."

4. **Constant competition with everyone:** A bit of competition can be a very motivating experience. Yet constant, intense rivalry can support a destructive level of internal competition, focusing attention and energy away from business goals. For example, the U.S. National Academy of Sciences surveyed all of the research on organizational team building strategies (Druckman and Bjork 1994). The strategies they surveyed attempted to get members of work teams to bond, collaborate, and work efficiently toward common goals by competing with other teams. When

the Academy released its findings, it was not surprising to learn that many of the most popular team-building programs had succeeded in increasing collaboration and cooperation between team members, but the teams were competing in a nearly suicidal fashion with other teams in the same organization. This type of misdirected, competitive behavior at work happens in many contexts. Analyze the total system and consider the impact of unintended side effects of encouraging wide-scale competition.

5. **Negative, critical, biased, and prejudicial feedback:** Some managers believe that in order to keep people on their toes, they have to watch carefully until people make a mistake and then jump on them, or remind them of their past mistakes when they are acting independently or seem satisfied with something they've done. When faced with this kind of feedback, many people either react with anger or feel depressed about constant criticism and stop trying.

Negative emotion is one of the biggest killers of motivation. A recent international review of performance feedback research studies (Kluger and DiNisi 1998) found that feedback that was critical of the individual actually depressed performance. This happened in one-third of all feedback research studies conducted both in natural settings and in the laboratory. In another third of the studies, performance feedback had no impact. In only one-third of the studies did feedback increase performance. When feedback emphasizes the performer's negative qualities, performance deteriorates. The finding that feedback resulted in negative or no consequences in two-thirds of all well-planned research studies suggests that it may even be more prevalent in practice since researchers tend to select typical strategies to test in experiments.

While a discussion of what kills motivation is a negative exercise, it is critical to emphasize that many common and popular features of organizations are doing much to hurt the work motivation of employees. The discussion turns next to the active ingredients of products that are designed to increase and enhance motivation.

Increasing Motivation

What are the factors that influence work goal choice, persistence, and mental effort? Motivation research tends to be fragmented, with different research laboratories emphasizing only one or two factors for investigation. In our discussion, we focus on research that has attempted to pull together the various approaches into a synthesized view (see Hardt and Rodin 1999; Ford 1992; Klein et al. 1999). The four factors mentioned by a number of independent research groups are:

1. Personal and team confidence;

2. Beliefs about organizational and environmental barriers to achieving goals;

3. The emotional climate people experience in their work environment;

4. The personal and team values for their performance goals.

Keep in mind that the gap analysis procedure in chapter 3 permitted you to get information on how much each of these pressure points was influencing a performance gap. Each of these factors is thought to have a major influence on choice, persistence, and mental effort.

FACTOR 1

Help people develop self- and team-confidence in work skills.

A primary motivational goal is to support a high level of personal confidence in employees about their own ability to achieve specific performance goals. People's belief about whether they have the skills required to succeed is perhaps the most important factor in their commitment to work tasks and the quality and quantity of mental effort people invest in their work. It is important to focus self-confidence on specific types of tasks. General self-confidence is not as critical for work motivation as is task-specific confidence (Bandura 1997).

When people do not believe they can succeed at a specific goal, they will not choose to tackle it. If they have started to work on the goal, they may convince themselves to switch to less important tasks or invest very little mental effort. (Remember though, that if people are overconfident, they will not invest much mental effort in tasks and also not take responsibility when they fail or make mistakes.)

Ways to increase confidence: The first consideration is to make certain that we constantly check with people to learn what they think will help them build confidence. The real danger here is that we tend to believe that others are like us and so will respond positively to the confidence builders that we prefer. The safest assumption is that people are *not* like us. Assume that other people are most likely to be motivated by very different values than our own, remembering that others' values are not wrong or stupid, only different. The most motivating attitude toward other people's values is understanding and respect. We do not have to share values or even agree with other people to respect their right to hold different beliefs and styles.

Keep in mind that as confidence increases, commitment to performance goals also increases. When you are selecting products or services that motivate people, they should include all or some of the following best strategies (Locke and Latham 1990; Bandura 1997) for helping people increase personal confidence:

INDIVIDUAL CONFIDENCE BUILDERS

- Assign specific, short-term, and challenging but achievable goals. Give people ownership of goals. Persistence is greater when goals are challenging, current, concrete, and possible to achieve. Impossible goals destroy commitment.

- Provide a way for people to get information, job aids, or training that is directly relevant to their goals if they must have additional knowledge and skills to achieve performance goals.

- Catch people doing a good job or making progress on a very challenging task and compliment them. Focus positive feedback on ability and effort. ("You are very good at this kind of task" and "You must have worked very hard.") Do not give compliments for performance on easy tasks.

- Focus corrective feedback on the faulty strategy, not on the person who used a faulty strategy. ("That approach did not work, let's look again at the goal and talk about some alternatives.") Do not make people feel wrong or inadequate; instead ask them to consider more effective ways to achieve a performance goal.

- Remember people's past successes and point them out when they face similar tasks.

- When interacting with others, project your own genuine expectation that they will succeed. If you do not expect them to succeed, you may be (or may become) part of their problem.

- Listen empathetically and actively when people describe their problems and gripes. You do not have to agree with them, but you must convince them that you understand what they are saying from their point of view. Accurately and neutrally paraphrase their view back to them and ask them if you understand them correctly *before* you give any advice.

Team Confidence

Team confidence is much more than the sum of individual team members' confidence levels. Team members must also believe in their colleagues and in collaboration. First, they must believe their colleagues collectively possess the skills necessary to achieve the team's performance goals. Perceptions that one or more members have weaknesses that may prevent team success depress team persistence. Second, each team member must believe that the entire team can cooperate and collaborate enough to accomplish team goals (Bandura 1997). If either of these two conditions is not met, teams will be distracted and delay or avoid achieving their goals.

In addition, people tend not to work as hard in teams (10 to 20 percent less) as they do when alone unless individual performance is monitored. This phenomenon is well-known in research and is called "social loafing." Group cohesion or team-building can be developed reliably and productively through focusing on successfully achieving authentic, short-term, and challenging goals that involve everyone on the team. The fun-and-games approaches, such as weekend survival courses, might be better experienced as mini-vacations rather than primary team-building methods.

TEAM CONFIDENCE BUILDERS

- Clearly describe the skills required to achieve the team's performance goals and point out that different team members have different but required skills. Make certain that everyone understands that the team possesses all of the necessary skills to achieve the goal. They must have confidence in each other as well as confidence in themselves.

- Provide individual monitoring and performance feedback for all team members to prevent "social loafing" during performance.

- Stay alert and quickly correct any intra-team coordination problems. Discourage unhealthy competition between team members.

- Apply all of the individual confidence suggestions to the entire team.

Handling Extreme Under-confidence

No matter how much confidence support is provided, everyone experiences confidence crises about some tasks or in some situations. Under-confidence is a work barrier only when people are avoiding important work tasks and/or making mistakes. Some people constantly complain that they lack confidence but do a solid job. This is not a problem. Avoiding work because of confidence issues *is* a problem.

There is some evidence that telling under-confident people not to worry so much or that they can do it is not very helpful. What the research seems to suggest in this instance is that extremely under-confident people need to hear advice and get support in ways such as: "Break the task into smaller chunks and take it step-by-step" and "We will give you help getting started." Do not do their work for them; give them supportive coaching about how to tackle smaller chunks and give support when they need it (Bandura 1997; Clark 1998).

Handling Extreme Overconfidence

One of the most under-recognized motivational problems at work is the destructive effect of overconfidence. Overconfident people assume that they have strong skills when, in fact, their ability level is inadequate for the task they face. They misjudge their own ability and the novelty of the tasks they face. When they receive corrective feedback about their performance problem, they reject responsibility for the failure. Worse yet, they also reject suggestions for alternative ways to approach the task. In a recent study by Hill (2000), managers tended not only to be overconfident, but not to adjust their overconfidence much when their failures were pointed out to them. So what approach helps a person adjust a destructive level of overconfidence?

It does not help to point out the overconfident person's incompetencies (although you might be tempted). The trick again is to focus on the strategy used and not on the person. The overconfident person must accept that the problem was caused by their approach, not by the person who evaluated their performance or by the way that the task or goal was set up. Sometimes it helps to point out that other people have succeeded at the task using a different approach. In extreme cases, it helps to set up a test of their approach and show them that it does not work. How far we go to adjust overconfidence depends, to a great extent, on the destructive potential of the problem.

FACTOR 2

Be alert and remove perceived organizational barriers to goal achievement.

People who have adequate confidence in themselves and their team may believe that they will be prevented from achieving goals by organizational barriers in the form of wrong policy, faulty or missing work processes, a lack of tools or materials, inadequate work facilities, and/or bias and prejudice (see chapter 6 for an extensive discussion of these issues).

Imagine what happens when sales incentives do not support policies about products that are supposed to be highest priority for sales staff. When instructions are given to emphasize one product or service line, but formal (or informal) incentives give more support for pushing another line, the conflict serves as a major barrier to implementing sales policy.

Faulty or missing work processes and procedures can cause confusion, waste, missed production deadlines, and a variety of other problems. Policies implemented to solve one problem can often cause unintended and worse problems elsewhere in a complex system. Employees, particularly women and minorities, are naturally concerned about the effects of bias or prejudice on the amount, quality, and timing of their opportunities and support level. Regardless of whether a perceived barrier is objectively verifiable or "imagined," it must be treated as a barrier to performance. People will not make a serious commitment to performance goals if they perceive barriers. Policy, procedure, work process, equipment, and material barriers are relatively easy to remove. Bias and prejudice barriers are more subtle and difficult to handle. The key ingredient in this barrier to work commitment is to convince people that the system is fair and that barriers to their performance goals will be removed or neutralized. Foster a climate of honesty, fairness, equity, and trust so that people will have less opportunity to believe that prejudice or bias will prevent them from goal achievement or recognition.

FACTOR 3

Create a positive emotional environment for individuals and teams at work.

Positive emotions, such as happiness and joy, support work commitment. Negative emotions, such as anger and depression, kill it. Yet it is not necessary for everyone to be happy in order to be committed. It is more important that people are not excessively unhappy, angry, or depressed about work issues. Anger and depression focuses our attention on past negative events instead of future goals. Naturally, organizations will benefit from helping people maintain the level of positive emotion that supports their maximum commitment. The effort invested in creating a positive, enjoyable work climate can pay off in increased work commitment for many people because the result is less negativity about work.

Yet different people sometimes have very different ideas about what encourages positive emotions or helps to get rid of negative feelings. Even if people were more alike, we cannot always do a great deal to modify extremely negative work emotions. Emotions are not always event-based. Some people simply react more quickly than others to routine events they perceive as negative. Bower (1995) has surveyed the research on the impact of a positive mood on performance. The research he reviews could be summarized as recommending the following ways to support positive emotions toward work:

WAYS TO CREATE A POSITIVE EMOTIONAL ENVIRONMENT AT WORK

- Engage people in decisions about the aesthetic design of their collective workplace. Invest in a bright, lively, positive environmental design.

- Let people decorate their personal work space (and themselves) if the decoration will not interfere with other people or violate important organizational policy.

- Allow people to listen to music while they work if listening does not decrease work efficiency or interfere with others' work.

- Eliminate rules and policies that reduce work enjoyment without providing a measured benefit that is greater than the loss of commitment they cause. Ask people what policies, if modified, would increase their enjoyment.

- Encourage everyone, including supervisors and managers, to be enthusiastic, positive, and supportive. Cynical, negative, pessimistic, and "sour grape" styles may be fashionable in some organizational cultures, but they do not encourage positive emotion or work commitment.

FACTOR 4

Suggest reasons and values for performance goals.

Earlier in this chapter we discussed effectiveness beliefs and their impact on performance. All of the advice on motivation up to this point can be viewed as ways to enhance the belief that commitment to performance goals will result in greater effectiveness. Confidence and emotions are intimately connected with effectiveness beliefs. Our confidence is a measure of our belief in our own abilities. Some of our strong emotions are the product of our reasoning and experience about how effective we have been and will continue to be in our work environment.

Values are one of the three powerful ways people express their views about what they expect will make them effective. People value what they believe helps them, and they reject what they believe stands in their way. Values can be viewed as preferences that lead people to adopt a course of action and persist in the face of distractions. Different people have different values. Yet research on values and performance suggests that there may be ways to identify types of values and connect them to work goals. The goal here is to increase people's work commitment by suggesting connections between their values and the benefit of achieving work goals. Eccles and Wigfield (1995) present evidence that most people use three different types of values:

1. **Interest value**. People will more easily and quickly choose to do what interests them the most. Many people are generally interested in mastering a new skill or adding to their expertise. This more intrinsic interest pattern often characterizes the most effective workers. Others are more interested in impressing managers with their capability. This more performance-oriented style can also be useful under some conditions.

   - Suggest connections between performance goals and people's interests whenever possible. Suggest that their goals represent an opportunity to do something that interests them such as master a new area or get a manager's attention.

2. Skill value. Most people seem more willing to do those things that they believe challenge one of their special skills. People who see themselves as analytical like brain teasers and difficult analytical problems and tasks. People who see themselves as artistic and style-conscious like tasks that involve aesthetic decisions and design challenges.

- Suggest connections between performance goals and people's abilities by suggesting that they are good at a certain kind of task and that it is an opportunity for them to show their skills.

3. Utility value. Much of what we do is chosen not because we love it or excel at it, but because we want the benefits that come when we finish. Utility value asks people to focus on the benefits of finishing the task and not on their lack of interest or discomfort about the means to reach the end. It is one of the ways we justify enduring something we do not like in order to get something we do like or avoid something that would be worse.

- Describe realistic benefits of completing a less desired task or goal and the risks of avoiding it. Do not inflate either the benefits or the risks.

Included in utility value is the highly contentious area of tangible incentives. The question here is whether offering people pay or gifts tied to exceptional performance actually motivates people beyond the type of strategies already described. The overall results of the large body of studies that are published in reputable journals follows (Bonner et al. 2000; Pendergast 1999; Pelham and Neter 1995).

To most researchers, the evidence is clear that financial or other tangible incentives (for example, vacations or luxury gifts) can significantly increase people's willingness to choose and persist at work goals. For the incentives to provide maximum benefit, the performance level must be very challenging, but not impossible. An impossible task is usually defined as one where the probability of success is less than fifteen percent. The conditions where tangible incentives seem to have the greatest impact on performance are:

- **Quota schemes**. When organizations use a "quota scheme," they appear to get the largest motivational benefit. Quotas offer additional bonus pay for work that exceeds a previous level achieved by the individual, team, or organization, or by another organization.

- **Piece-rate schemes**. The second most effective use of tangible incentives is in "piece-rate" schemes where a set amount of output (for example, the manual assembly of one electronics board) is tied to a set rate of pay. Quota and piece-rate schemes are often combined to get the benefit of both approaches.

- **Tournament schemes**. The third ranking incentive approach is "tournament schemes" where pay is linked to performance rankings based on competition between people doing the same job. This plan is often used to motivate sales staff. One factor that is thought to diminish the effects of tournament incentives is the fact that only capable people tend to participate (those who feel they will not win tend to avoid this kind of scheme, and so it may attract only top performers and overconfident people). Another problem here is that competition sometimes leads to attempts to sabotage the efforts of competitors, thus reducing the overall benefit to the organization.

- **Flat-rate schemes**. Fixed pay schemes are the least effective overall. It is ironic that work for a set salary is the best example of a flat-rate incentive system. Here we pay people for full-time work, usually pegged at forty hours a week. Very few studies have found motivational advantages for the most common tangible incentive system used worldwide.

Disputes about Incentive Systems

Many of the disputes about pay incentives focus on evidence, drawn largely from classroom studies involving children, that personal interest in work tasks decreases when tangible incentives are used as a reward. The argument is that paying people to do what they should do because they are interested in the job switches their motivation away from a fascination with the task and focuses it on the pay they are promised for performance. In the future, the argument goes, people who are paid more for interesting work will work for extra pay and not because they are interested. The best advice in that situation is to withhold tangible incentives from people who are already achieving business goals on their own, unless there is an excellent financial reason to exceed business goals at the possible risk of future "interest" motivation.

Another argument concerns the contrast to the "informational" function of *intangible* incentives such as pats on the back (what some call "catching people doing a good job"), recognition award plaques, and "performer of the week/month/year" recognition. In general, intangible incentives are thought to work because when we are acknowledged for good work, the acknowledgment gives us information about how to be successful. Some motivation experts suggest that tangible awards, when they are misapplied, simply serve very expensive informational functions that could be achieved without paying people more.

FIGURE 5.2: JOB AID
DIAGNOSING AND SOLVING MOTIVATION PROBLEMS

Problem:
Buy-in
Avoiding task
Delaying
Refusing
Procrastinating
Arguing
Intending

Behavior:
Rejects or avoids task commitment, easily distractable in the face of barriers, may try to shift task to someone else, may complain about assignment. May "intend" to pursue goal but not actively choose to do it.

Motive:
Perceives task as having negative or no impact on success or control. Believes acceptance of task will reduce success. May believe that task is impossible or irrelevant.

Solutions: Create value to get buy-in:
- Describe later utility
- Connect to interests
- "You are good at this"
- Remove negatives
- Provide incentives
- Describe risk of avoiding
- Get agreement with task
- Keep mood positive
- Give C^3 goals (see chapter 2)
- Ensure trust and fairness

Problem:
Overconfident
Failing at task or making mistakes
Avoids responsibility
Blames others

Behavior:
Overconfident, values task but uses wrong approach to solving problems, so fails or performs poorly—then blames others.

Motive:
Perceives task or problem as "familiar" when it is, in fact, novel and requires much thought and effort to handle.

Solutions: Adjust belief about task:
- Show novelty & difficulty
- Test their approach
- Validate required approach
- Attribute mistakes to effort
- Request new approach
- Monitor progress closely
- Give feedback

Problem:
Under-confident
Failing at task or making serious mistakes
Anxious about failing
Blame themselves

Behavior:
Under-confident, avoids task
Easily distracted by another task
May try to find honorable way out

Motive:
Perceives self as unable and/or environment as preventing success. Believes that failure will lower self-esteem and organizational perceptions of competence.

Solutons: Reduce challenge by focusing on the task:
- Give clear goals
- Break task into parts
- Provide procedural advice
- Attribute failure to effort
- Attribute success to ability
- Monitor closely
- Give feedback

Finally, some people argue that tangible incentives imply that people are permitted not to achieve the goals attached to the incentive. The argument is that offering people money or gifts beyond salary for specific achievement implies that the task being promoted can be avoided—that people can opt not to work toward those goals. Some people apparently believe that incentives are offered to get them to do something that they do not have to do and that they are allowed to give up the incentive rather than invest effort in the task.

WHEN TO USE TANGIBLE INCENTIVES

- Use incentive schemes to achieve challenging but possible goals and never with either easily achieved or impossible stretch goals.

- The most effective tangible incentive schemes are quota schemes where people are rewarded for exceeding a set level of performance (either their own past performance or a benchmarked level from organizational leaders). Quota schemes are even more effective if there are added incentives for bigger units of exceeded performance.

- Competitive or "tournament" schemes can bring positive results provided that everyone participates and that sabotage of top performers is discouraged.

- The least effective incentive scheme is the fixed rate of pay for a unit of time—our most common "salary or hourly" schemes.

- Make certain that you implement incentive schemes carefully. Most seem to fail because they are poorly designed and haphazardly implemented, not because the incentive fails to motivate people.

Conclusion

The current "cognitive" research on work motivation is one of the largely unexplored resources for increasing performance. Many of the gaps between current performance and the levels required to achieve business goals are caused by a lack of motivation, not a lack of knowledge and skills.

Very few of the recommendations for these motivational approaches cost very much. Even the tangible incentive programs described can be very cost-effective when used properly. Most of the newer motivation builders ask organizations to foster a culture where positive beliefs, expectations, and practices are encouraged. The objective of adopting a more positive motivational climate is to increase individual and team confidence, interpersonal and organizational trust, collaborative spirit, optimism, positive emotions, and values about work. The benefit of achieving a more motivated organization is in increased persistence at work tasks and a higher quality of mental effort invested in work goals.

Remember that the result of gap analysis is most often a mix of motivational programs. This mix must be designed, developed, and implemented to close the gap or achieve a stretch goal. We recommend waiting to design motivational programs for employees until these programs can be fully integrated with knowledge and organizational process and material changes. Wait for implementation until you have finished the complete analysis of all solutions. Fully integrated performance improvement programs are more effective, much more efficient (Fuller and Farrington 1999), and considerably easier to evaluate.

To this point, we have presented research-based ways to support knowledge and motivation—two of the three factors that influence performance at work. The next chapter presents the third and final factor, the structure of the organization. It will cover the factors that influence all organizations, as well as how different organizational structures require different types of performance support.

Additional Resources on Performance Research

Topic: *Motivation for Work; Motivation Theory; Motivation Research*

Bandura, Albert. 1997. *Self-efficacy: The exercise of control*. New York: W.H. Freeman.

Clark, Richard E. 1998. Motivating performance. *Performance Improvement* 37, no. 8: 39-47.

Ford, Martin E. 1992. *Motivating humans: Goals, emotions and personal agency beliefs*. Newberry Park, CA: Sage.

Karau, Steven J., and Kip D. Williams. 1995. Social loafing: Research findings, implications, and future directions. *Current Directions* 4: 134-139.

Locke, Edwin A., and Gary P. Latham. 1990. *A theory of goal setting and task performance*. Englewood Cliffs, NJ: Prentice-Hall.

Pintrich, Paul R., and Dale H. Schunk. 1966. *Motivation in education: Theory, research and applications*. Englewood Cliffs, NJ: Merrill.

Williams, Kip D., and Steven J. Karau. 1991. Social loafing and social compensation: The effects of expectations of coworker performance. *Journal of Personality and Social Psychology* 61: 570-581.

6

Organizational Gaps: Alignment, Culture, and Change

THE THIRD AND FINAL CAUSE of performance gaps is the lack of efficient and effective organizational work processes and material resources. Even for people with top motivation and exceptional knowledge and skills, missing or inadequate processes and materials can prevent the achievement of performance goals. We begin by defining organizational processes and material resources, along with the related concepts of value chains and value streams. We then describe the current research findings on the active ingredients of effective work processes and materials handling issues. There are more elements to ensuring effective organizational support, however, than efficient processes or materials. Organizational culture inevitably filters and affects all attempts to improve performance, and successful performance improvement will depend on taking the specific organizational culture into account. We present a method for developing a cultural profile of any organization.

103

Any time an organization changes a work process, employees' jobs are changed. What is organizational change if it is not changing how people do their jobs? There is currently a great deal of interest in the effectiveness of organizational change processes, and with that in mind, we will survey the research findings on the success rate of popular change processes such as the quality movement, downsizing, reengineering, team-based work, horizontal organizations made up of partnerships, and special variations such as skunk works and pulsating organizations.

Work Process: All organizational goals are achieved by a system of interacting processes that require specialized knowledge, skills, and motivation to operate successfully. These work processes specify how people, equipment, and materials must link and interact over time to produce some desired result. Familiar examples of processes are manufacturing (including sub-processes such as assembly and equipment maintenance) and human resources (including sub-processes such as hiring and payroll). When these processes are inadequate or misaligned with business goals, the risk of failure is great. If organizational policies fail to support processes, the result can be chaos and inefficiency. Even workers with adequate knowledge, skills, and top motivation will not succeed to close performance gaps and achieve business goals when faced with inefficient work processes.

The redesign of work processes (with accompanying adjustments in knowledge, skills, and motivation) has resulted in a number of extraordinary achievements in different industries. For example, Harley-Davidson reduced the manufacturing time for their motorcycle frames from seventy-two days to two days and increased their quality rating of finished frames from about 50 percent up to nearly 100 percent (O'Neal and Bertrand 1991). Many information technology organizations have adopted a rapid application and development (RAD) process for building applications and have chopped their development time from an average of twenty-four months to less than four months (Martin 1991). Iomega, faced with an unacceptably long 28-day manufacturing cycle for hard drives, reduced that time to thirty-six hours. The process changes that accomplished this feat for Iomega also reduced its inventory and rejection rate dramatically (Business Week Editors 1994).

Where procedures tell individuals how to do something, processes tell groups of teams or individuals how to combine their separate work procedures into a smooth functioning unit. Part of the performance improvement task is to identify and fix process barriers.

Material Resources: Organizations also require tangible supplies and equipment to achieve goals. The design and availability of tools and material supplies for work has been an issue for many hundreds of years, so the temptation is to overlook it as a cause of performance gaps. It should not be discounted. Manufacturing organizations require a great variety of equipment (including specialized environments and buildings) and material resources to achieve process goals and to aid individuals and teams as they perform essential procedures. The material resources for knowledge work include various types of essential and rapidly changing information technology, along with the more routine types of office supplies and equipment. For example, when Iomega reduced its manufacturing cycle for its hard drives from twenty-eight days to thirty-six hours, a key component in the savings was the discovery of an unexpected equipment problem in the final stages of the assembly process.

Value Chains and Value Streams: Much of the interest in materials availability and work process redesign has come out of an organizational development area most often called "value streams" and "value chains." Value streams are a form of analysis that describes how an organization's departments and divisions interact and what processes they implement. The goal is to understand how the business as a whole works and the cost-effectiveness of different work processes. It also identifies the processes that are most influential in achieving business goals. Value stream analysis helps describe work processes in the same way that cognitive task analysis (chapter 4) captures advanced knowledge and skills of individual experts.

Value chains are more limited than value streams. Chains use the information from streams to identify the way that divisional or team processes achieve goals for internal and external customers. For example, a value chain for improving the reactions of customers with quality complaints might draw on the value stream description of marketing and sales, order fulfillment, and customer services. Value streams can be very inefficient (because they require the smooth interaction between separate and sometimes disconnected divisions in an organization). Consequently, they operate very slowly and are costly. Value chains help clarify the critical, client-focused objectives and the processes that exist to achieve more limited goals. See page 106 for examples of value stream and value chain analysis in Europe and North America.

Identifying Organizational Causes in Gap Analysis

The goal of conducting interviews and focus groups and studying work records is to collect the views of people who must close the performance gaps. Whenever people tell you about formal or informal organizational policies, processes, or resource levels that prevent the closing of a gap, classify their comments as organizational barriers. All aspects of the organization's work processes or policies that prevent or delay work goal achievement must be noted and checked for validation.

Since some people typically attribute their problems to some aspect of the organization, and since many people would rather be thought to be critical rather

THE CONSEQUENCES OF RELUCTANCE
TO ANALYZE VALUE STREAMS

Naomi Garnett, a lecturer at the University of Reading in the UK, has provided a very interesting "action research" account of the efforts to introduce value stream process analysis and organizational change in the UK construction industry in the 1990s. The account is available in the report of the annual conference held by the International Group for Lean Construction (IGLC) at the University of California at Berkeley in 1999 (http://www.ce.berkeley.edu/~tommelein/IGLC-7/PDF/Garnett.pdf).

Garnett describes the problems with adopting some of the gap analysis techniques recommended in this book. Specifically, she argues that building trades in the UK are reluctant to invest the up-front effort required to analyze the process barriers preventing efficient achievement of business goals. The reluctance, she argues, focuses on an unwillingness to invest the time and expense required to perform gap and process analysis. She contrasts this reluctance with the acceptance of these processes in a number of North American organizations that have succeeded in achieving dramatic cost reductions while increasing production and customer satisfaction. She argues that these savings have been the direct result of leaner processes resulting from revised value chains.

UK industry managers were reluctant to believe that changes in their costing structures and contractual arrangements with suppliers could result in major efficiencies. They insisted on quick-fix strategies that did not pay off and used the lack of results from ineffective analysis to support their reluctance to invest in longer-term, systematic analysis of gaps and causes. UK managers also wanted cost-saving estimates ahead of agreeing to invest in gap analysis, and when told that estimates had to follow analysis, they often resisted.

The result, in Garnett's view, is a sector of the UK economy that will not change quickly and will fall behind in competitive advantage. She offers the very interesting opinion that the culture of some industries makes it very difficult to accept evidence that easily persuades managers in other industries.

Value stream analysis and mapping strategies have been recently clarified in a book by Rother and Schook (1998). An analysis of their approach to industrial engineering can be viewed at: http://www-iwse.eng.ohio-state.edu/~fmpf/Proposal%20-%20Sadono.htm.

than uninformed or unmotivated, interview data has to be checked for accuracy. For example, a person may claim he does not know how to do a job. However, if you ask follow-up questions requesting examples, this person may end up telling you about a gap in an essential work process. If you ask for details when a person claims that her manager discourages her work, then you may learn about delays in the availability of essential tools or supplies. Examples of work process barriers are issues such as inadequate, inefficient, missing, or conflicting policies and processes, and/or the unavailability of needed tools or materials.

Simple process defects or the need for routine supplies are easy to fix. Yet because all organizations are complex systems, many performance gaps tend to be interconnected. When a problem pops up in one part of the system, its cause can sometimes be found in a different part of the system. Similarly, when you start to implement a performance improvement solution that you believe will close a performance gap in one area, your solution might cause a problem in another area of the organization.

There are two poorly understood reasons for this complexity. First, many performance improvement specialists fail to realize that all organizations are systems that have their own culture. Second, change is so pervasive in today's organizations that special attention must be given to performance issues that result from change processes. Adding to the difficulty is that culture and change processes often interact, sometimes in destructive ways and sometimes in positive ways. Some organizational cultures foster specific types of performance problems and are more compatible with certain types of performance solutions and change strategies.

Organizational Culture

Who said "We don't know who discovered water, but it was most likely not a fish"? The water we swim in at work is, to some extent, the culture of our organization. Work culture is present in our conscious and unconscious understanding of who we are, what we value, and how we do what we do as an organization. In many ways, organizational culture is the most important "work process" in all organizations because it dictates how we work together to get our job done.

Organizations develop different cultures over time. Consider the difference between an investment banking firm, such as Salomon Brothers or Goldman Sachs, and a commercial bank, such as Bank One or Wells Fargo (Deal and Kennedy 1999). The investment banking culture is a high adrenaline world of high risks, quick feedback, and big rewards. These companies accordingly have flat, highly fluid structures to allow for career mobility, and teams are generally organized around short-term deals. New associates are recruited from top-tier business schools and highly selective colleges and are already members of an elite; their socialization into the world of executive suites, exclusive clubs, and expensive resorts will increase this sense of elitism. They are given immediate and none-too-gentle feedback on their performance and paid a lot of money based on short-term tangible results.

Even though a commercial bank is also a financial institution, the two worlds and two cultures are very different. The commercial bank is a much more team-oriented world of deliberate process and much slower feedback. Commercial banks have more hierarchy and more rigid structures and are organized around types of customers or types of financial services. New bankers are often recruited from good regional business schools and local universities, many coming from the ranks of the accounting departments, which also pre-selects for deliberate, practical, stolid people. Careers are slower to develop and less risky, feedback is more oblique and based on more qualitative factors, and the pay is good, but not mind-boggling.

As an example, despite their surface similarities, investment banking and commercial banking are two entirely different cultures and have different structures, procedures, processes, people, metrics, and incentive systems. When Bank of America acquired Charles Schwab's brokerage firm, the merger looked good on paper; the two both dealt in retail financial services and had overlapping retail customer bases who wanted both product lines. However, it never worked in practice—the two cultures were incompatible. The investment bankers kept double parking their Ferraris in the spaces reserved for the commercial banker's Mercedes, figuratively speaking. A few years later, Charles Schwab reacquired the firm and went private again. On the other hand, Citibank and Traveler's Insurance have relatively compatible cultures, structures, processes, and people, and hence better odds on the long-term survival of their merger.

Culture and Performance in Different Organizations

Culture is a way to describe the core values, goals, beliefs, emotions, and processes learned as people develop over time in our family and in our work environments. Most people in organizations are members of many different cultures. Our background and current lives include membership in different national, regional, work, religion, political, and family groups as well as differences in gender, age and professional identities. Culture is both a powerful force in performance and a difficult characteristic to identify and to influence. There are three common approaches to culture in organizations.

1. Culture in the Environment

Some people view culture as being in the organization or environment. This view focuses on how, for example, the organizational culture of Royal Dutch Shell might shape a different performance style for employees than, for example, the culture of Microsoft. This approach studies how developing and changing the culture of the organization can change performance. People in this area often work from case studies describing how organizational culture changed performance in desirable ways. People in this area believe that cultural patterns can be changed by changing the work environment.

2. Culture in Groups

Others view culture as the property of groups of people, but not individuals or environments. This view often leads, for example, to discussions about the cultural differences between Japanese and European workers, or the different expectations and values of Hispanic and Near Eastern cultural traditions at work. Many of those who have grown up in "I" cultures have learned to place a premium on individual initiative, responsibility, and competition. Those who grew up in a number of "We" cultures tend to place a premium on cooperative group activity, shared responsibility, and consensus. "I" culture people will, under some organizational culture conditions, act like "We" culture people. The relatively recent transition to a team focus and complex patterns of partnership and collaboration in Western business is an example of how organizational culture sometimes moderates national culture patterns. Eastern "We" culture people will act like "I" culture individuals under some conditions. People from "We" culture traditions learn, for example, to compete in sales organizations that value individual initiative and competition. In all of these views, the underlying goal is to try to identify "leverage points" where cultural patterns can be selected (through hiring and promotion) and utilized or, if necessary, modified (through training, social experiences, and job assignments) and focused on the achievement of organizational goals.

In most discussions it is recognized that organizations sometimes suffer from clashes between the many different cultural beliefs and expectations of the people who work in them. People in this area believe that cultural patterns can be changed by changing the beliefs and knowledge of groups of people at work.

3. Culture in Individuals

The view presented in this book is a bit iconoclastic. It is more helpful in performance improvement to think about a person's "work culture" as an important part of their core knowledge about two things: what work processes are effective for them and how and why they do things, and each person's distinctly different motivational patterns about what their skills are, what is worth doing, and what makes them successful. These beliefs, which many of us accurately attribute to our life experiences, influence most of our individual decisions and actions—often in unconscious ways.

The suggestions made in this chapter for ways to handle culture in organizations emphasize the "unconscious" aspects of culturally learned knowledge and motivational patterns. So much of our cultural heritage is expressed automatically and unconsciously that our cultural self-awareness is very limited. As was pointed out in chapters 3 and 4, about 70–90 percent of all of our knowledge and skills are automated and unconscious. Our cultural knowledge may stretch to the 90 percent unconscious level. Therefore, in order to influence performance, performance specialists often have to modify both the organizational environment and the knowledge, skills, and motivational approach of the people who work in them. Enhancing, using, or changing cultural influences on work can be accomplished in exactly the same way as using or changing any other kind of performance knowledge or motivation. Thus, in our view, training and motivational programs are, by definition, attempts to transmit new organizational culture and change people's cultural behaviors at work.

Most of us are tempted to draw on our knowledge about a person's nationality, race, religion, or past employment to anticipate their reactions to personal or work events. This approach is simply unreliable, and it tends to be disrespectful to individuals and groups. People within the same national group (or religion or gender or racial identity group) are very different from each other. Stereotyping is wrong, and it does not work. For example, even if people born and raised in Japan tend to have learned "we" culture values, they do not always react to work events in a "we" fashion. People born and raised in North America do not always act in an individualistic, competitive fashion. Yet people who, for example, react with "we" values on one set of work tasks are likely to continue to apply the same values to other work tasks.

It is important to encourage everyone to replace cultural (and racial, gender, age, or any other) stereotypes with a more reliable and powerful way to describe the effects of the unique cultural habits and beliefs adopted by each individual during their life long development. Such a system is not available yet. As was explained in the introduction, it is distressing that research on the very popular Myers-Briggs instrument indicates that the test is not reliable or valid. In North America, the Myers-Briggs test has tended to replace cultural stereotypes with Myers-Briggs stereotypes. Neither approach is reliable or valid, and both tend to label people and place them into rigid boxes. There are a number of attempts underway in different fields to replace the Myers-Briggs with more reliable instruments that accurately predict performance under specified conditions. For example, the American Psychological Association has recently developed the "Big Five" measures of personality and style. One of those measures, "Conscientiousness" (the extent to which someone is dependable, thorough, reliable, and uses solid planning processes versus people who are more careless, negligent, and unreliable), has been found to predict exceptional performance at work (Pervin and John 1999). The other four measures in this series tap "Agreeableness" (people who tend to be more kind, trusting, and warm versus those who are more selfish, distrustful, and cold); "Extroversion" (those who are more assertive, talkative, and have a high activity level versus those who are more reserved, silent, and passive); "Emotional Stability" (people who are more relaxed and on an "even keel" versus those who are nervous and moody or temperamental); and "Openness to Experience" (people who show imagination, curiosity, and creativity versus people who are more shallow and "clueless"). See Goldberg (1993) for more information.

The key message here: do not use any psychological assessment of questionable validity for hiring, training, promotion, or retention. Using an invalid test for any of these reasons is legally indefensible and exposes your company to large lawsuits, not to mention very unfavorable publicity. The best people will not want to work for a company seen as manipulative, untrustworthy, and unfair. If you want to use the Big Five or any other assessment, work with consultants who have specialized training in psychological tests and solid experience evaluating test results and targeting them to specific work goals.

Our view is that personal "culture" is another way to describe a person's core knowledge and motivational patterns. Every individual is unique, regardless of their national heritage, family experiences, religion, race, and gender. Trying to influence performance by taking account of a person's national culture is, in our view, unlikely to be successful.

Developing an Organizational Culture Profile

The answers given by people to questions such as the following would all fall under the subject of organizational culture.

- In what ways is this organization different and unique?

- What aspects of your organization and its goals do people here value most?

- What is different about the way that you get your jobs done?

- How and when do you get performance feedback?

- When major changes are made, who drives the change and what typically happens?

- How and by whom are important decisions made in this organization?

Culture also involves beliefs about the importance of individual initiative and competition, and the value of group process and collaboration. Imagine comparing the answers to these questions by Microsoft employees to responses from Ford or General Motors employees. Imagine replies to the questions from a group of investment bankers and a group of commercial bank employees. Very different cultural profiles would emerge.

Since the causes and solutions to performance gaps must be translated so that they are compatible with the culture of an organization, it is necessary to create a cultural profile. One way to accomplish this goal is to identify and interview three or four bright and verbal people from different units in the organization who were hired recently—within the previous six months. New hires will not yet have become so familiar with the culture of the group that they are no longer aware of how they have changed their own patterns. Ask each person the questions above and note their answers. Interview people alone and compare answers. Significant differences may either point to areas where different units in larger organizations have different cultures or areas where you need to check further for a more accurate account. Examples of organizational culture profiles can be found in the case studies at the end of the book.

Aligning Organizational Culture with Organizational Behavior

It is not yet possible to use each individual's work culture to enhance their performance. What *is* possible is to use culture profiles to align the culture of any organization with all of the important policies, procedures, and communication within the organization. The core beliefs that characterize all organizational cultures can guide decisions about goal selection and the processes and procedures used to achieve those goals.

For example, in the past Hewlett Packard (HP) has placed a strong emphasis on valuing its people, and its internal communication suggests that sharing is central to the HP way: sharing in setting goals, sharing in hard work, sharing in stock ownership and the profits from success, and sharing in adversity (Packard 1995). In 1970, during a downturn in the US economy, Bill Hewlett and Dave Packard were faced with the prospect of a 10 percent employee layoff, the usual remedy, in order to remain solvent. They tried a different approach instead, and instituted the "nine-day fortnight" or a plan to share the burden of the economic recession. Everyone in the organization, from factory workers to senior management, worked nine days out of each two-week period. This resulted in a 10 percent reduction in the work schedule and a 10 percent reduction in the payroll. Everyone shared the pain of a 10 percent pay cut, but there was no layoff and six months later when order rate was up again, HP's workforce was intact and united. Even in the early 1990s, when downsizing was the hot management concept in the US, and HP, like many other companies, needed to reduce staff, HP made extraordinary efforts to accomplish this reduction through attrition, early-retirement programs, and voluntary severance with generous financial packages. Cultures can change, however, and there are indications that HP's organizational culture is doing just that: mandated pay cuts and large-scale layoffs were announced in mid-2001 in response to a slowing economy.

Contrast the traditional HP approach with the culture of the major American car companies twenty years ago, when even a temporary bulge in inventory meant prompt layoffs. The car companies paid well, but the relationship between the company and the employees was transactional (a fair wage for a fair day's work), rather than the relationship-oriented, almost familial relationship supported for many years at HP. The cultures are very different. The car companies are heavily unionized, with elaborate rules about roles and responsibilities and sharp status lines between labor and management. Contract negotiations were vehement contests of will, politics, and organizational skills. The unions grew up as a counterbalance to management, and the structure and processes of the car companies accommodated the yin-yang of these two organizational entities within the companies: work rules, seniority, grievances, shop stewards, and annual retooling shut downs all became part of the culture at the car companies.

When organizational goals, policies, or procedures conflict with organizational culture, expect performance problems. One of the most noted examples of this was the management style of "Chainsaw" Al Dunlap who applied what he termed his "Rambo" management style to downsizing as a business goal with vigor and relish. Dunlap believed most managers were too soft to achieve dramatic results. At Scott Paper, Dunlap laid off 11,200 workers to bring the company back to profitability and sold the company to Kimberly Clark for $7 billion in 1995. At Sunbeam, he closed sixteen factories, slashed corporate staff, and laid off 6000 employees in order to double operating earnings and bring the stock from $12.50 to $40. Dunlap drove his management team and the company relentlessly in an effort to cut costs and boost the stock price. He became an icon for the success of downsizing. After two years, the board raised his salary to $2 million a year and gave him $68 million in stock options. Three months later, he was abruptly fired over a weekend when the cumulative effect of his management style of intimidation and unrealistic expectations brought the company to the brink of implosion, combined with the surfacing of questionable accounting practices. The people at Sunbeam were exhausted by the threats and bullying, the extremely short-term perspective, and the highly irregular tactics to boost sales figures (such as counting appliances as sold today even though they would not be delivered for six months or paid for until six months after that).

The stabilizing force of culture can also work against the company's interests. For example, the president of a mid-size regional bank decided on goals of customer focus and satisfaction (Belasco 1990). He instituted a major advertising campaign and a large internal communication effort about his vision of "Your personal banker." At first, results were promising as new accounts rolled in, but after several months account closings and customer dissatisfaction were high. Upon investigation, the president discovered that while branch managers were pursuing new business and bringing in more new accounts, nothing was changing in the customer experience.

Tellers, the main customer contact point, continued to be treated as second-class citizens and in turn gave customers second-class service. The branch managers and officers who brought in new business ignored the new customers once they were in the door. A promising business initiative ran aground on the typical bank culture of that time when a bank regarded itself as an institution for serving business and wealthy individuals, while depositors were considered fortunate to be able to have their money handled by the bank.

Conversely, when management decisions are aligned with culture the results can be extraordinary. For example, Johnson & Johnson responded in accord with their corporate vision and culture during the Tylenol crisis in 1982 by recalling all of their product worldwide and replacing all products bought by customers. Even though they suffered a major financial setback, the company came through with a public relations and morale victory.

Aligning Organizational Culture with Organizational Policy and Procedures

Over time, people in organizations build up patterns of response to challenges. In the early life of a new organization, huge challenges often distract management from the deliberate design of an organizational culture. As organizations develop and confront challenges, its culture may change slowly and invisibly. Thus, patterns of dealing with important core issues become ingrained over time. Eventually, those ingrained patterns become automated. So while people are often aware of mission, goals, and formal policy in organizations, those items are the visible tip of the cultural iceberg. Most of the culture of many organizations is beneath the surface and so is implicit, unconscious, and automated. This more hidden culture can be found in our unconscious styles, attitudes, and behavior. It is also implicit in the operational patterns people develop and support at all levels. Thus, when people fail to get the necessary resources that were promised for a high priority work goal or when a policy is not supported by effective work processes or procedures, one of the possible causes is a conflict between some aspect of organizational culture and our current performance goals.

Organizational Culture and Change

Much of the strength and impact of modern organizations comes from a tension between stability and change. The need for a stable organizational culture and work processes that are compatible with work culture has to be constantly balanced with a need for flexibility to accommodate complex and rapid market shifts. Yet organizations that attempt to manage change by adopting one of the many processes available to them are faced with dismal evidence about success rates. The best evidence would support the generalization that nearly all available organizational development and change processes fail two out of every three times. The remainder of this chapter presents a scorecard reflecting the success of change processes. We suggest ways to maximize the positive evidence and make it work for you as you select change processes in the future.

Most of the discussions of how organizational development and improvement influences performance take a view from space, in which people attempt to assess the impact of forms such as virtual or team-based structures on factors like product and service quality, implementation speed, and profitability. The one negative aspect of an organizational factor point-of-view is the risk that performance specialists will forget that organizations are made up of people whose knowledge, skills, and motivation drive the organization. It is crucial to focus on people and what they need to succeed.

There is no best process for all organizations at all stages of development. All types of organizational structures and environments can have neutral, helpful, or destructive effects on human performance. What is accomplished at work is due in large measure to an interaction between the work environment and people's knowledge, skills, and motivation. It is important to know what types of knowledge, skills, and motivation people need to work in different types of organizations. How do different organizational types and processes help or hurt the day-to-day performance of the people who work in them? What types of support do people need to give their best performance when working in different organizational structures, cultures, and processes?

In this chapter we offer specific, research-based suggestions for ways that knowledge, skills, and motivation can provide maximum support for different types of organizational change. One of our goals is to ensure that change processes will succeed by suggesting ways to prepare people for change. The limited research available suggests that organizational development is more likely to succeed when people are equipped to handle its unique challenges.

Do Most Organizational Change Processes Succeed?

The first point to make about organizational research is that it is very rare. The National Research Council estimated that only about 3 percent of the published articles about organizational improvement report systematic empirical research (Druckman, Singer, and Van Cott 1997). This is a risky situation. History has demonstrated that when no systematic research is conducted on organizational processes, each new approach catches management attention for a brief time and quickly ends up in the trash can. This boom-and-bust cycle does not allow for organizational learning. The patterns that influence organizational productivity are ignored or forgotten.

Equally distressing are criticisms of the approaches that have been used to evaluate organizational change and improvement programs. In a review of the methodology of quality of work and empowerment research, Golembiewski and Sun (1990) and Newman, Edwards, and Raju (1989) found evidence for a positive-finding bias. Their reviews of many empowerment experiments indicate that the most positive results come from the most defective evaluation designs. This suggests that the evaluators have a bias toward evaluation conditions that emphasize positive results, but tend to ignore or downplay negative outcomes.

Most of the current arguments about the different processes for organizational design and change are based on case studies. These descriptions are offered as either cautionary or desirable examples, but they are not systematic studies with balanced evidence about change processes. When promises of dramatic productivity improvements are made on the basis of a few case studies, the results usually do not generalize between organizations. This is a destructive pattern that repeats itself constantly in the performance improvement field.

Most of the research surveying participants or comparing different types of programs has been conducted on processes such as Total Quality Management (TQM), downsizing, and reengineering. One reading of the evidence for the benefits of current organizational development and change processes is enough to depress even the most optimistic advocate. Here is a representative sample of the conclusions reached by the National Research Council's (NRC) review of the organizational effectiveness survey research (Druckman, Singer, and Van Cott 1997).

- More than two-thirds of all TQM projects studied are abandoned within two years due to a perceived lack of results (Druckman, Singer, and Van Cott 1997).

- A survey of Fortune 500 companies suggested that only 20 percent had achieved their quality objectives with TQM, while 40 percent said that TQM was a "complete flop" (Druckman, Singer, and Van Cott 1997).

- Only 9 percent of downsized companies report an increase in quality (Bennett 1991) and McKinley (1992) found that it generally increased costs, bureaucracy, and centralized decision-making and may have caused performance declines in most organizations.

- Three-fourths of the senior managers in downsized companies reported that trust, morale, and productivity suffered after downsizing (Henkoff 1990). Durable, long term negative effects on work motivation have been found in many studies (Druckman, Singer, and Van Cott 1997).

- A survey of corporate executives in six industrialized nations found that less than half of their downsized companies had achieved cost-cutting goals, and fewer had achieved operating objectives such as improved productivity (Swoboda 1995).

- The largest survey of reengineered organizations (500 US companies and 1200 European companies) indicated that 70-75 percent have attempted reengineering, and 85 percent who tried it found little or no gain from the effort. Half realized no market share gain (CSC Index 1994).

Choosing and implementing effective organizational change and improvement processes is one of the most important problems facing the international business community today. The introduction to this book described how NASA developed an approach to knowledge and skills that will benefit our effort to locate and develop research information to aid in the selection and development of organizational improvement processes (Druckman, Singer, and Van Cott 1997). The "known to be known" and "known to be unknown" types of knowledge are important to the fit between different organizations and improvement processes, and the support needed by the people who must make change work. So what is known now that can help make decisions?

Features of Effective Organizational Change and Improvement Programs

To begin, Dixon (1994) surveyed twenty-three reengineering projects to identify the factors that seemed to produce success. Their list might be the best overall set of recommendations for how to help organizational change processes succeed.

Six Types of Support Necessary for Most Organizational Change Processes

Dixon's study focused on organizations making changes in direction—those shifting their business processes to achieve improvement in efficiency, service, or quality. The focus of most of the projects surveyed was work process changes. Dixon found four factors that seemed to predict success in all of the projects they studied. In addition, we have included two points from the National Research Council findings.

1. **Have a clear vision, goals, and ways to measure progress**. The key elements for successful change are found in the connection between a compelling vision, a sound business process to reach that goal, clear work goals accompanied by effective work procedures, motivational support for everyone, and assessment of results that reflect both the achievement of the vision and connected business and work goals.

2. **Align the structures and the processes of the organization with goals.** Many of the documented failures in organizational change initiatives result from a failure to ensure that the structure of the organization and key business processes are in alignment with business goals. Resources such as Rummler and Brache (1995) provide an excellent overview of how to map an organization to ensure that they have accountable organizational resources and tested processes to produce the deliverables. If you change your goals, you need to review structure and processes and make any needed changes.

3. **Communicate constantly and candidly to those involved about plans and progress.** This conclusion turns up consistently in studies of effective performance enhancement projects. Clear and candid communication engenders trust and helps people adjust their performance to accommodate unexpected events. Trust increases the spread of commitment to change goals on all levels. The informational and corrective feedback components of communication help people adjust the knowledge and skills they are using to accomplish goals. This message needs to be repeated much more often than most of us realize. Coca-Cola, the most recognized brand name in the world, reportedly spends more than a billion dollars a year on awareness advertising.

4. **Top management must be continually involved in the improvement process.** The commitment and active involvement of top management is another universal factor that turns up in reviews of successful organizational change projects. Upper management vision and commitment, clearly and candidly communicated to everyone and demonstrated with visible management involvement in the process, is a critical success factor.

5. **Provide adequate knowledge, skills, and motivational support for everyone.** Change processes most often require training in teamwork and process analysis. Chapters 4 and 5 suggested that teamwork training should emphasize at least three types of content: first, the new knowledge and skills that are needed to achieve change goals; second, the coordination skills needed to get team work accomplished efficiently and without conflict; and third, techniques that build trust by team members in the importance of the separate skills of their colleagues. Team members often fail to understand that each individual might be contributing different skills to the achievement of team work goals. It is also important that individual contributions to teamwork be assessed to avoid social loafing.

6. **Caution! All change processes with the same name are not equal.** Imagine trying to give advice about cars if every vehicle called a Ford Mustang was actually a different vehicle with different engineering specifications? Too often people who report using similar change processes are actually using very different procedures and processes. The American Quality Foundation surveyed companies that used TQM and found more than 900 different tactics and tools that were all called TQM. Similar questions have been raised about most of the mainstream approaches to organizational change. The evidence suggests that everything called reengineering, TQM, job redesign, or downsizing has not used consistent processes in all, or even most, applications.

Use extreme care when selecting specific change processes to achieve organizational goals. The same care must be exercised when generalizing about the effectiveness of different approaches. It is wise to look beyond labels and always ask for a clear description of the procedures and processes that were actually used in successful performance improvement projects. Our definitions of these different approaches are drawn from Druckman, Singer, and Van Cott (1997).

Each change process may require its own unique mix of performance support tools. While the six points described above seem to apply to all change processes, there is evidence that each of them (TQM, downsizing, and reengineering) needs specific types of knowledge and motivational support to enhance success.

TQM requires clear tactics, strong commitment, and cognitive task analysis. The essence of TQM seems to be the establishment and maintenance of replicable procedures that produce quality. Since everyone tends to perform similar jobs in different ways, the development of standard procedures often threatens individual and team performers. Trying to establish one best way to accomplish a familiar goal requires many people to change their own familiar approach and adopt the new standardized approach. Like a golfer with a new putting stance or a different swing, accuracy and motivation suffer while new procedures are becoming familiar and automated with practice.

Organizations using this approach must be constantly alert to maintain everyone's commitment. Another challenge brought on by TQM is connected to the development of clear procedures. As we capture the processes and procedures that produce quality in an organization, we need to be constantly alert to the 50 percent error rate of experts who describe how they do what they do so well.

Downsizing must be accomplished with candor and outplacement support. Research on downsizing strongly suggests that some of the negative results reported in the research can be overcome with candor (the clear and candid communication suggestion made in point 2 above) and aggressive counseling, job retraining, and outplacement support. The combination of these factors have been found to be the difference between the huge number of failed downsizing projects and the minority of successful attempts (see studies by Cameron et al. 1993; Schweiger and DeNisi 1991).

Radical organizational reengineering may be nearly impossible. Occasionally research shows that certain approaches simply do not work when applied in a short timeframe. Radical reengineering may be a case in point. Nearly all of the reviews of the research on the effects of this approach indicate that it simply does not work when radical change is attempted within a short time span. On the other hand, incremental reengineering change that is introduced with a long-term plan and adequate performance support seems to have a better chance of success. Another alternative is to simply spin off a new organization and start with a new culture from the onset. Inertia and resistance to change are very strong in some areas of an organization. When resistance is strong, it seems better to bypass the areas of highest resistance and apply incremental change first in areas that are most flexible and supportive. Smaller successes tend to pave the way for more extensive application of change over time. In this regard, the National Research Council suggests that organizations think of sequencing all organizational change activities: "The three processes range from an emphasis on smaller (downsizing) to an emphasis on better (reengineering) to an emphasis on being perfect (TQM)....moving from efficiency (downsizing) to effectiveness (reengineering) to excellence (TQM) can be seen as a...progression" (Druckman, Singer, and Van Cott 1997, 63).

Different Types of Organizations Require Different Types of Performance Support

Besides the different performance support needs for specific types of organizational change processes, different types of organizations also require different types of support. While most organizations must deal with constant change, people in different types of organizations often need very different support to handle both dramatic change and routine challenges. The needs of people in a virtual organization of partnerships would be very different from the needs of people in a more bureaucratic organization. If the special mix of knowledge, skills, and motivation required by each type of organization is provided, the performance of those organizations should increase and the need for radical change should decrease.

Team-Based Organizations

Team-based organizations need motivation, feedback, and access to expert skills. There are many varieties of ways to organize teams and focus their effort. Regardless of the type of team, each person must believe that other team members have all of the separate skills required to achieve the team's goals and will cooperate to achieve them. Confidence in team member skills is usually enhanced if just-in-time (JIT) training and/or expert coaches are available to give skill support. Collaboration and motivation are enhanced if each team member's contribution is assessed separately and candid but supportive feedback is provided about collaboration. Compensation of team members becomes a major issue if members doubt each other's skill or commitment. Without individual assessment and feedback, team confidence is lower and social loafing tends to occur. Teams must maintain a delicate balance between individual initiative and collaboration. Teams must also guard against destructive competition with other teams in the same organization (chapter 2).

Network or Virtual Organizations

Network or virtual organizations need clear coordination and the basis for trust. An increase in specialization and the need to provide a wide range of services and products to customers has led to more networked or virtual organizations. Each member organization can focus on its core competencies and yet still offer a wide range of services in collaboration with other organizations or teams. These inter-organizational or partnership arrangements challenge the trust of members. Today people work together across great distances and boundaries, whether geographic, organizational, or professional. Sometimes they are collaborating on a project with colleagues who were competitors only a few weeks ago, and may be customers a few weeks from now. Professionals in such organizations need assurances that collaborative agreements will be maintained. This is the inter-organizational form of the fair collaboration issue that faces all teams. Members of these virtual organizations also require highly-developed coordination support.

Horizontal Organizations

Horizontal organizations require clear and formalized procedures. In response to the need for greater efficiency, faster decisions, and speedy implementation, organizations are becoming flatter. As middle management is eliminated, the need for coordination of work flow across functions is increased. Often this responsibility falls to line managers who have no influence over their counterparts as work is handed off and processed by different teams. While many line managers are able to collaborate with their counterparts, complex jobs and the tendency for independent action often undermines smooth coordination. Thus people in horizontal organizations need very clear and formal procedures for coordination and accountability.

Pulsating Organizations

Pulsating organizations need incentives to stop when the job is finished. Many organizations are set up to handle seasonal events such as holiday sales, special events, or short-term jobs. These organizations are designed to be temporary, but the people in them often form strong bonds and a sense of pride in their accomplishments. This leads group members to resist disbanding and invest effort in the survival of the group. Investing effort in ensuring the survival of the organization after its initial goal is accomplished sometimes overwhelms the task at hand. Supporting people who work in pulsating organizations requires a plan to provide incentives to disband the team when the goal is accomplished. The types of support required are similar to those recommended for downsized organizations—aggressive outplacement and candid exchanges of information.

Skunk Works Teams

Skunk works teams need highly skilled members and training. Some teams are directed to operate outside of organizational culture and rules to accomplish important and complex, but poorly-defined, goals. For example, in the aeronautics industry, skunk works teams have been formed to solve major problems in the design of military and commercial aircraft and space vehicles. In theory, skunk works groups can circumvent the bureaucratic rules that stifle creative problem-solving. Evidence about this kind of team suggests that only the most capable people can work in them, and the teams need access to first rate training and coaching from top experts.

Conclusion

At the beginning of this chapter, we described the need for efficient and effective organizational work processes and material resources that support the achievement of business goals. Missing or faulty processes and inadequate materials are often the cause of barriers to the achievement of performance goals, even for people with top motivation and exceptional knowledge and skills. Suggestions were made for identifying and correcting faulty or missing work process and/or necessary equipment and materials that are barriers to closing performance gaps.

To extend the discussion of work processes into areas that are currently challenging businesses, we then turned to a discussion of the impact of organizational culture on work processes, and finally to the impact of popular organizational change processes.

All change programs seem to require a number of similar types of support. Essential change-supportive processes include selecting change processes with proven track records, providing a clear future vision and performance goals, measuring progress, communicating constantly with everyone about progress and problems, involving top management at all stages, and providing the skills and knowledge necessary to successfully implement and track results. Other types of organizational change support should be determined, in part, by specific types of change goals, the type of organizational culture making the change, and the unique skills and motivation of the people involved. For example, major change in team-based and/or virtual organizations made up of both "I" culture and "We" culture people require special types of support. Teams in these types of organizations would require ongoing motivational support so that they will continue to value the process and maintain trust in, and smooth collaboration with, their coworkers.

One way to judge the importance of an issue is the amount of research support invested in advancing our knowledge about it. Almost every authority on organizations agrees that managing effective change is one of the very highest priorities of all successful organizations. Yet an effective system for organizational change and development will continue to be elusive until more systematic research is conducted. At the moment, those responsible for change initiatives seem content with case study information about other people's experience with a change process. Yet success stories about someone else's organization cannot be generalized for your organization. If someone reports that a process worked for Microsoft or General Motors, that report does not mean that the same or similar process will work for you, even if you are in the same industry. Maximizing the one-third success rate means drawing on the results of carefully planned research and applying it in a setting where results are evaluated continually so that mistakes can be corrected.

Remember that the result of gap analysis is most often a mix of organizational process and work material programs. This mix must be designed, developed, and implemented to close the gap or achieve a stretch goal. We recommend waiting to design organizational change programs for employees until these programs can be fully integrated with knowledge and motivational changes. Wait for implementation until you have finished the complete analysis of all solutions to gaps and stretch goals. Fully integrated performance improvement programs are more effective, much more efficient, and considerably easier to evaluate.

The discussion turns next to evaluation, one of the most important, yet underutilized, performance improvement tools. Chapter 7 describes ways to measure and validate attempts to close performance gaps.

Additional Resources on Performance Research

Topic: *Organizational Change; Organizational Culture; Work Processes; Organizational Factors in Performance*

Druckman, Daniel, Jerome E. Singer, and Harold Van Cott, eds. 1997. *Enhancing organizational performance*. Washington, D.C.: National Academy Press.

Galbraith, Jay. 1995. *Designing organizations: An executive briefing on strategy, structure and processes*. San Francisco: Jossey-Bass.

Golembiewski, Robert T., and Ben-Chu Sun. 1990. Positive-finding bias in QWL studies: Rigor and outcomes in a large sample. *Journal of Management* 16: 665-674.

Newman, G. A., J. E. Edwards, and N. S. Raju. 1989. Organizational development interventions: A meta-analysis of their effects on satisfaction and other attitudes. *Personnel Psychology* 42: 461-489.

Rother, Mike, and John Shook. 1998. *Learning to see: Value stream mapping to create value and Eliminate Muda*, v.1.1. Brookline, MA: The Lean Enterprise Institute.

Schweiger, David M., and Angelo S. DeNisi. 1991. Communication with employees following a merger: A longitudinal field experiment. *Academy of Management Journal* 34: 110-135.

7

Evaluation and Cost-Benefit: Assessing Progress and Results

EVALUATION IS an absolutely essential ingredient when you are attempting to close performance gaps or improve performance. It is the only way to determine the connections between performance gaps, improvement programs, and cost-effectiveness. Evaluation is one of the most cost-effective activities in performance improvement, because it is the one activity that, if applied correctly, can ensure success. It is often resisted, however, because of the fear that it could document failure. Evaluation is the process that helps us make decisions about the value of all of the activities we've described over the course of the book. It is the only process that will give us an objective view of our progress toward closing performance gaps. Without systematic evaluation we are left with "wishful thinking" or self-serving impressions that are often wrong and sometimes dangerous.

A number of years ago, we encountered a graduate student with a major evaluation problem. As part of his masters program in training and development, "Jake" had been working as an intern with a very large company (let's call them "Stack Training, Inc.") that provided external training design and delivery services to large corporations. Jake came to an academic progress meeting with his university advisor and confessed that his manager at STI had demanded that he falsify evaluation data about a major training product that was being delivered to one of the Fortune 100 companies.

Jake was given the impression by his STI supervisor that it happens all the time. When he expressed reluctance, he was warned that if he refused he would "not get a job in this town and maybe not in this business—anywhere." Through a strange twist of fate, this very unhappy situation actually had a happy ending. Jake was advised to first use some of the newer evaluation analysis techniques to check to see if the evaluation in question was actually negative.

He learned that the analysis method STI had used originally had masked positive results of an effective training program. This allowed everyone involved to work over time to correct the integrity problem at STI (only one of its managers seemed inclined to falsify evaluation results, and eventually he was fired). STI reacted to the problem by working harder at evaluation and eventually earned a reputation for objective and accurate product assessment. Jake went on to a very successful career as a training manger.

This tale emphasizes two of the most troubling aspects of evaluation. First, even though accurate and positive evaluation is the basis for making the most informed and successful decisions about performance, the simple yet powerful tools for evaluating performance are seldom used or are not implemented correctly. Second, negative results, if viewed as personally threatening, can occasionally lead people to desperate measures or to avoid evaluation altogether.

This chapter demonstrates a relatively simple, cost-effective, and successful approach to performance evaluation that leads to positive situations, not to mistakes, threats, or career damage. Learning what to evaluate and how evaluation should be conducted are vital components of successful performance improvement programs. Even when you use research-tested active ingredients when designing or selecting programs, you need to ensure their fit with your organization and your work goals. Evaluation can help you edit and tune programs to maximize payoff. Thus the objective of this chapter is to describe the most powerful, inexpensive, and efficient ways to determine with accuracy whether you reach your goals, and whether you do so cost-effectively.

Evaluation: An Essential Element of Success

Managers who would not consider making a business decision without accounting or marketing data sometimes make critical performance decisions without any information beyond a guess. Many performance improvement specialists say privately that, in the past, very few of their clients have evaluated projects in ways that helped them succeed. Many factors lead to this oversight, including cost, time pressures, and the fear that a negative result will cause problems. There is some evidence that this pattern is changing. Interest in transfer and return on investment evaluation is growing at a rapid pace. Evaluation can be very cost-effective and essential to success, and more performance improvement specialists and managers are making it a routine part of their activities.

All evaluation studies must satisfy two criteria: reliability and validity. Establishing these criteria upfront will help you communicate your expectations to evaluation specialists and vendors who conduct studies for you. Reliability, the simpler of the two, requires that all evaluation methods give the same results each time we measure. This protects you against measures that change constantly and produce different results every time they are used, because of the measuring instrument. Reliability is relatively easy to achieve, yet its importance is often overlooked. We need only to develop specific procedures and instruments for measuring the aspects of performance and goal achievement that are important to us. Then we need to standardize those procedures so that they measure in the same way every time. Standards can be changed later to reflect improved methods. Developing instruments and standard ways of administering them is much simpler than it sounds. These activities can be perfectly compatible with the way that most performance improvement projects are designed and administered.

The second criterion, validity, requires that all evaluation measure exactly and only what it is supposed to be measuring. This criterion is the one most often violated in performance assessment. For example, if we attempt to measure the amount of knowledge employees gain in a training course with a reaction form that asks them how much they learned, the results will indicate how much employees *think* they learned, not how much they actually learned. Reaction forms tell us whether trainees liked or valued training or the trainer. Reaction forms too often report high amounts of learning when little occurred and vice versa (Clark 1982). Thus training reaction evaluation could be reliable but not valid in these cases, because the actual results were the opposite of what the invalid instrument reliably reported. If the instrument reported the same invalid result each time it was used, it is still reliable—which is why we need both reliability and validity for all evaluation activities. An example of a valid measurement of learning would be a problem-solving exercise or memory test (provided they represented the knowledge and skills the trainees learned during training). The more that we make use of research evidence about the event being measured, the better our chances for validity. One performance evaluation system that supports this point of view is the Kirkpatrick model.

Four Levels of Evaluation

Many specialists have found great value in the use of a performance evaluation system designed in the 1950s by Don Kirkpatrick (Kirkpatrick 1998). He described a four-level evaluation system that handles most of the questions anyone may want to ask about training systems. This chapter presents a slight modification to his system to support the evaluation of all performance support systems. Kirkpatrick's evaluation model has the benefit of nearly a half century of use in many different organizational settings in different countries and cultures. It is still the preferred approach for most trainers. While there have been many improvements suggested about "how" to evaluate each level he recommends, the Kirkpatrick basic four-level model is still the best and almost universally used system. In brief, our expanded model looks like this:

Figure 7.1
Four Levels of Evaluation

LEVEL 1: Reactions
Are the participants motivated by the program? Do they value it?

LEVEL 2: Impact During the Program
Is the system effective while it is being implemented?

LEVEL 3: Transfer
Does the program continue to be effective after it is implemented?

LEVEL 4: Bottom Line
Has the transfer contributed to the achievement of organizational goals?

© 2002 CEP Press

Ask consultants or vendors to use this system for early and mid-course trial-and-revise "formative" evaluation, in addition to end-of-project evaluations. Recent work on the four levels has focused on level four, usually to extend our tool kit for measuring the financial impact or ROI (return on investment) from performance improvement programs (Phillips 1997). Since the measurement of any one of the four levels can turn up negative results that may be balanced by positive results on other levels, it is critical to measure all levels if possible.

LEVEL 1

Check *reactions* (motivation) of participants toward the performance program.

Reaction evaluation is usually conducted with a few questions that ask participants whether they like and value the program. These questions can be asked before a program starts (to determine expectations for the program and pre-program levels of performance), during a program (in order for changes to be made in time to achieve positive results), and at the end of a program (to be subtracted from the "before" data to get a measure of gain and a summary judgment about the program's motivational impact on participants). Figure 7.2 gives some examples of reaction questions. Most experienced performance consultants strongly advise soliciting anonymous information; candor is more important than tracing reactions to individuals. If it is necessary to compare "before and after" reactions, it is still possible to mark responses without tying them to specific individuals.

A combination of one or two open-ended questions where participants can tell you something you did not expect is very effective. For example, "What would you change about this program to make it more effective for you and others?" and "What do/did you value most about this program?" In addition, it is valuable to have closed questions where participants are asked to quantify their reactions. These quantified reactions can be used to compare early, mid-course, and summary judgments of programs, to change unsuccessful elements of a program in mid-course, and to compare the motivational reactions of different groups to the same program.

Notice that the questions in figure 7.2 follow the recommendations given in chapter 5 on motivation. Since reaction forms measure the motivational qualities of performance improvement programs, we must measure the reactions that are motivational in nature—values, emotional reactions, self-confidence—and their impact on persistence and mental effort.

Keep in mind that positive Level 1 results indicate only that people are motivated to persist and to invest effort in the performance program. Positive reactions do not indicate whether they gained anything useful or will use information after the program is finished. Reaction information also does not tell you whether a successful program will support your organizational goals. Reactions can be highly positive and the program still can have negative or damaging results. The benefit of Level 1 information is that it tells you about the motivational impact on the participants.

What choice would you make if Level 1 reactions were very negative but the other three levels were highly positive? This might happen if the program is difficult and requires a great deal of effort to master or if the ideas challenge conventional beliefs or expectations. One approach is to re-frame the issue by featuring the

---

Figure 7.2

Examples of Level 1 Reaction Questions

Open Questions

What would you change about this program, and how would you change it, to make it more effective for you and for others?

What features of this program do/did you like or value most?

What do/did you dislike about this program?

Closed Questions

Please circle the number that best represents your own reactions to this program:

Far Below Average—1
Below Average—2
Average—3
Above Average—4
Far Above Average—5

1 Overall, how much are/did you enjoy(ing) this program (compared with other, similar programs)?	1	2	3	4	5
2 Will you be able to use what you gained on the job (will you be supported in using it on your job)?	1	2	3	4	5
3 How confident are you that these strategies will work (will what you gained be effective when you use it)?	1	2	3	4	5
4 How much do you value the goals of this program (compared to other performance goals you face)?	1	2	3	4	5

challenge of the program in a positive light. For example, some technology training courses have begun to call themselves "boot camps," alerting people to their difficulty but suggesting their importance for anyone who wants to advance in this area.

LEVEL 2

Check the learning/motivation/organizational change *impact* during the program.

Level 2 evaluation targets the impact of all programs while they are being implemented. If a knowledge gap is being closed with a training program, this level examines the learning that takes place during the training course. If improved performance requires motivational or organizational change, this level measures the progress of changes taking place. If a performance improvement program gets off track, Level 2 serves as an early warning and an opportunity to make corrections.

Level 2 evaluations should focus on the thing that is the central focus of each performance improvement program. In a training class, for example, you would need to see a person perform the skill in question. Since "doing" is procedural in nature, the assessment of learning during training is relatively simple. You merely need to engage the learners in practice exercises where they apply what is being learned. At the same time, score the practice exercises as a gauge of what they have learned up to that point. For procedural skills, have a trained observer (or computer) use a checklist containing the key elements of the procedure to assess learner proficiency. Scores on these progress checks can be used to diagnose and correct learning problems or training presentation glitches.

Any exercise or checklist used for Level 2 assessment should be based on the task analysis used to design the training. In the task analysis, you have assembled all of the information you need to make a Level 2 evaluation checklist. For assessing procedural skill, evaluators simply transfer the individual steps in all procedures taught in the training to a checklist format. Include a place on the checklist where observers can indicate whether each trainee has performed all of the steps accurately during practice.

Notice that on the example procedural checklist in figure 7.3, there is a space at the bottom where an expert can indicate whether the person's performance meets overall expectations for adequate mastery of the procedure. The combination of procedure-based checklists and an expert's judgment is a better evaluation of Level 2 or Level 3 than either type of assessment alone.

Practice exercises serve a double purpose. The more practice trainees experience during a training course, the better able they are to learn and transfer the knowledge and skills back to the job. Practice promotes (but does not guarantee) both learning and transfer. Practice exercises can also be designed to increase people's enjoyment of training. Some people wonder why computer-based training hasn't been quicker to adapt very powerful simulation technology, such as that used in flight trainers or SimCity for practice exercises. These simulations are activity-based, so they encourage relevant practice while making use of the capacity of computers to provide engaging, information-rich displays.

Practice Formatted as Games

While fun is good, formatting practice exercises as games can backfire. All new learning and performance changes require considerable mental effort on the part of all participants. Mental effort can be enjoyable. Yet there is good evidence that when

Figure 7.3

Level 2 Checklist for Training on Medical Procedure

ITEM: Central Venus Catheter Placement for Rapid Infusion of Fluids During Surgery	Not Done Or Done Incorrectly	Done Correctly
1 Selected catheter appropriate for condition		x
2 Placed patient in appropriate position		x
3 Sterilized the site using appropriate technique		x
4 Injected 1% Lidocaine		x
5 Located correct point for needle insertion		x
6 Started insertion with 2-hand technique		x
7 Created anatomical position with non-dominant hand	x	
8 Stabilized syringe when reaching for wire		x
9 Used correct technique for advancing wire into needle		x
10 Advanced wire to correct depth		x
11 Used appropriate scalpel technique to incise skin (0.5 cm)	x	
12 Introduced dilator appropriately into the incision		x
13 Advanced the catheter correctly into the incision		x
14 Maintained guide wire positioning w/ non-dominant hand		x
15 Positioned catheter at the correct depth		x
16 Withdrew the guide wire		x
17 Prepared the lumen(s) correctly		x
18 Attached fluids to the catheter correctly		x
19 Attached the line using non-absorbable sutures		x

Maximum Score Possible: **(19)**

Trainee's Score on this assessment: **2 (done incorrectly)   17 (done correctly)**

In my judgment, this trainee:

Can perform the procedure adequately_____   Needs more practice__x__

Comments: *Practice steps 7 and 11 then repeat exercise until successful.*

Examiner's Name _____*JR*_____

practice is formatted as games, sometimes participants do not invest adequate mental effort, reducing or eliminating the performance impact of practice (Salomon 1983, 1984). Apparently people expect games to require less mental effort than other types of problem-solving exercises. Pre-testing practice exercises before they are offered will reduce or eliminate this pitfall by balancing the work and entertainment components of practice.

Level 2 Cautions

In the past, the evaluation of learning during training has most often been accomplished either with reaction forms or with memory tests in multiple choice or fill-in-the-blank formats. Neither type of test indicates learning in its fullest sense. Learning is best assessed by asking someone to apply what they have learned (Resnick 1987) and explain why they are doing it (Van Merrienboer 1997). The two most common test formats are typical features of most of the new computer-based training systems. Asking someone to memorize and describe a procedure on a test does not guarantee that they will be able to perform the procedure they have described on or off the job. In fact, almost anyone can memorize a procedure successfully but not be able to perform it. Look at the medical procedure in figure 7.3 as an example, and ask yourself how long it would take you to memorize the nineteen steps. When you could repeat the steps from memory, would your successful memory test indicate that you could perform the surgical procedure? Memory might be a good test of some learning in formal university education, but increasingly, even schools are de-emphasizing memorizing concepts in favor of analysis and inquiry skills that emphasize the application of more complex concepts to problem-solving (Bransford et al. 1999; Resnick 1987; National Research Council 1996). Certainly most jobs require that we be able to do something other than memorize and repeat information, and most jobs do not rely on the employee memorizing large amounts of knowledge. The exception can be found in sales. Customers expect sales people to have a great number of facts about products at their fingertips. Memory for product features is assumed to represent expertise on the part of the salesperson. Thus sales training sometimes requires a test of memory for new product features.

Checklists for Organizational Change Programs

When assessing organizational change programs, we only need to collect information about the indicators you or your vendor described when the program was being designed. Change assessment at Level 2 requires another checklist based on the milestones in your timetable. Each time a milestone is reached, the progress measurement is entered into the checklist. If you have set clear progress goals and have concrete ways to measure goal achievement, then the checklist serves as a progress indicator. If your assessment indicates that the amount of goal achievement is less than desired, then the information helps make in-progress adjustments to get a program back on track.

For example, chapter 2 discussed customer service as one of the factors essential to business success. Customer satisfaction can be a vague and elusive concept. Your evaluators need to know what you did to drive up customer satisfaction. Businesses such as banks and fast food companies have very high numbers of customer transactions and have extensive research on what customers want. These industries tend to distill that research into a set of high-impact practices. That explains why, for example, well-trained fast food employees look at you and smile before taking your order, and why bank tellers use your name sometime during your transaction. Earle and Keen (2000), in their analysis of successful businesses, provide the following set of practices that lead to greater customer satisfaction and repeat business in e-commerce.

Figure 7.4		
Example of Customer Satisfaction Survey at Level 2		
Was the customer offered information on related products?	Y	N
Did the customer receive a follow-up marketing offer?	Y	N
Were marketing communications personalized?	Y	N
Were repeat buyers recognized?	Y	N
Did the customer receive responses to questions?	Y	N

© 2002 CEP Press

Surveys containing questions similar to those above can easily be turned into an organizational audit of specific behaviors and used as the basis for evaluating organizational change, motivational programs, and training, where needed. For example, remembering to offer customers information on related products would not require much learning, but would require practice and feedback until the behavior became a regular practice. On the other hand, personalizing marketing communications might require additional training on techniques for tailoring material for the individual needs of a customer. Beyond that, recognizing repeat customers might involve linking a technique such as a club card or customer number to special offers or discounts.

LEVEL 3

Check performance improvement transfer and durability after program.

It seems reasonable to assume that if reactions to a performance improvement program are totally positive and the program achieves its goals when it is implemented, we should see ongoing positive results of these gains after the program is completed. In fact, performance can decrease over time when both Level 1 and 2 indicators are positive. Level 3 evaluation checks to see whether gains made during a program persisted after the program's completion.

Ongoing change evaluation: Because the longer term impact of organizational change programs is so negative, it is essential to track the impact of change programs after they have been implemented. If you have developed and used a tracking system for Level 2 evaluation, the same assessment can be used for spot checks after the program is fully implemented. People tend to revert to previous patterns until new learning becomes stronger than old habits. Check monthly or quarterly to determine whether changes are holding up and contributing to improved performance. Many changes require new behaviors on the part of people who implement them. Many performance improvement specialists describe personal experiences with very expensive change programs that succeed initially, only to revert back after an initial rush of enthusiasm. Investing in ongoing monitoring of the transfer and persistence of change programs is absolutely necessary, given the evidence about their long term durability.

Transfer of training evaluation: Nearly all training programs, whether off-site, on-the-job, or web-based, suffer from a lack of transfer (Ford and Weissbein 1997). Before people enter training, their managers must communicate their clear expectations that the knowledge and skills learned in training will be applied as soon as they finish a course. Many trainees interviewed after training say that they were either discouraged from using new knowledge and skills or get the impression that no one cares. If managers communicate clear expectations that trained people will apply new knowledge and skills, trainees will be more motivated to transfer what they have learned. Managers who are on-site a few days after people exit training to ask about transfer experiences are providing the motivational support necessary for the training investment to pay off.

Another vital transfer-enhancing strategy is to ensure that the knowledge and skills taught in the training course are in a form that can be applied on the job. This may seem obvious, but many transfer problems result from teaching the wrong type of knowledge in training courses. For example, some training courses require people to memorize the steps in complex procedures, instead of asking them to practice the procedures. Other courses simply show trainees the features of a new technology rather than demonstrate how to use it on the job. If the knowledge you teach is not related to the job people are doing, you will get no transfer.

Finally, you can evaluate transfer by interviewing or surveying a sample of the people who completed the training, their managers, and their subordinates or others who are affected by the new knowledge and skills. Ask people for on-the-job examples of how the application of the knowledge and skills learned in training solved a problem or accomplished a task. These success stories are valuable insights about transfer and can be used as concrete examples of the value of training. Transfer evaluation itself is a reminder to trained staff that they are expected to use what they have learned. Survey questions for those trained include items such as: "Are you now doing anything different on the job now as a result of attending the training program?" If the answer is no, ask why. If the answer is yes, ask them to describe what they are doing differently and its impact on their job.

The most valuable transfer evaluation responses come from those who observe or collaborate with trained people. Managers, supervisors, and co-workers who observe the daily work of trained people are often in a good position to judge the effectiveness of transfer because they see how often and how effectively new knowledge and skills are being used. Organizational data collected as part of the monitoring of work products is also a source of transfer information. If data about the speed, accuracy, number, and quality of work is collected, it is often useful to check that data before and after a performance improvement program for evidence of transfer.

The extent of your evaluation activities should be determined by the size and importance of the training program. For less important programs, survey questionnaires or interviews can ask observers questions such as how many coworkers completed the training, whether they've observed the application of new skills by those coworkers, and what types of examples they can give of their coworkers' use of those skills. The more extensive or important programs require more transfer effort— including a) use a control group of similar employees who have not yet been trained; b) get 100 percent response from a randomly selected sample or the entire group of trained people and observers; c) repeat the evaluation over time to ensure that the transfer stays in place; and d) try to find concrete work products that reflect the use of (or failure to use) the new knowledge and skills.

Finally, keep in mind that transfer of knowledge and skills can be wildly successful, yet the impact on the greater business goal can be zero or negative.

LEVEL 4

Check the bottom line impact of changes on organizational goals.

If they were forced to emphasize only one of the four levels, most managers would choose bottom line evaluation. Bottom line evaluation answers the question of whether the program made any difference to the business or other organizational goal achievement. This level of evaluation is arguably the most expensive and difficult to conduct, and there are two conditions in which organizations should not attempt it.

First, if there is no evidence of tangible results and/or the transfer of these results in Level 2 or 3 evaluations, it makes no sense to examine the effects of the program on the bottom line. The second reason to avoid bottom line evaluation is when organizations are unwilling to implement change programs in a way that facilitates bottom line evaluation. In general, you can check the bottom line impact of any program, provided you implement it in different divisions or locations of the same organization at different times. Measuring impact at three locations is the ideal for this design. The result will give you information about the exact contribution of the performance improvement to closing the gap and influencing the bottom line indicators that represent organizational goals. In fact, the design is so comprehensive that it can be used to efficiently measure all four levels of impact at once.

Staged Innovation Design

The staged innovation design (Clark and Snow 1975) is the only comprehensive design for level four evaluation if organizations want to ensure that the program in question, and not something else, was the cause of measured changes in the bottom line. This kind of design has been around for many years, but is not well known outside of a few evaluation specialists. Figure 7. 5 provides a graphic representation of the design.

Let's say that we identify three divisions where a new performance improvement program will be implemented. Collect baseline data on the gap at all three locations to determine the pre-program level of performance. In figure 7.5, Level 1 is called "baseline," Level 2 is "performance," Level 3 is "transfer," and Level 4 is "impact." The evaluation design gives you solid data on the extent of the problem to be solved at each site prior to its introduction (so that later you can accurately estimate the extent of the change). As the program is presented in the first location, collect reaction, change, and transfer data. After the first introduction of the program, you can make trial-and-revise changes that improve it based on the reactions of participants and the changes that resulted. Improvements can then be incorporated into the program that is presented at the next location (Location B in Figure 7.5). When you present

Figure 7.5

Bottom Line Staged Innovation Evaluation Design

First Trial Application of a New Program

	Level 1 Baseline Measure	Level 2 Performance Improvement	Level 3 Transfer Test	Level 4 Impact Measures
Location A	X	O	X	X
Location B	X		X	X
Location C	X		X	X

Second Application—Revised Program

*(This version begins after the first trial is finished
and the program is improved if necessary.)*

	Level 1 Baseline Measure	Level 2 Performance Improvement	Level 3 Transfer Test	Level 4 Impact Measures
Location A	X		X	X
Location B	X	O^2	X	X
Location C	X		X	X

Third Application

	Level 1 Baseline Measure	Level 2 Performance Improvement	Level 3 Transfer Test	Level 4 Impact Measures
Location A	X		X	X
Location B	X		X	X
Location C	X	O^3	X	X

FIGURE LEGEND:

X = Test of performance at one of the four levels (Level 1: Reactions measured by baseline tests; Level 2: Change measured by performance improvement tests; Level 3: Transfer measured by transfer tests; Level 4: Organizational goal change indicated by impact measures).

O = Original program implementation at first (A) site.

O^2/O^3 = Revised and improved versions of the original program at site B (O^2), site C (O^3), and so on.

© 2002 CEP Press

the program for the second time, however, you *continue* to measure impact at the first location (this is a transfer measure and evidence about the "durability" of the program over time after it is introduced). You again collect a pre-program baseline at Location C (to make certain that something has not changed that will dilute or enhance the program effects artificially).

A great number of questions can be answered by the staged innovation design for evaluating the bottom line impact of programs. First, you determine whether there are differences between locations by simply looking at the difference between the baseline measures taken before the change program is introduced. Second, you assess the relative impact of the program at different sites on participant reactions, learning and change, and transfer of impact. You can also change the program to make it more generally effective after you assess its impact at the first and second location. Third, you get solid evidence about the long-term impact of a program (and the presenters of the program) over time at two different sites because you continue to measure at location A and B after the programs are finished. Finally, you learn the real impact of the program on the bottom line and can assess costs and benefits more accurately.

Interestingly, many organizations that evaluate do make changes in response to their findings but fail to be systematic about it. This design has the virtue of letting you evaluate which changes make a difference. Otherwise, your modifications may be without direction, or you may repeat earlier problems with a revised but equally ineffective program.

Conclusion

Evaluation is the way to support our judgments about whether something is worthwhile. It is an absolutely necessary component of all successful performance improvement efforts. Evaluation provides us with reliable and valid information about the initial state of the system we are trying to change, the progress of our attempts to change it, and the bottom line impact of the change on business goals. Evaluation can also help us make mid-course corrections in performance improvement programs to increase their impact and protect your investment.

Additional Resources on Performance Research

Topic: *Evaluation of Performance Improvement Programs; Evaluation Designs; Training Evaluation; Cost-benefit and Cost-effectiveness Evaluation*

Kirkpatrick, Donald L. 1998. *Evaluating training programs: The four levels.* San Francisco: Barrett-Koehler Publishers.

Morrow, C., M. Jarrett, and M. Rupinsky. 1997. An investigation of the effect and economic utility of corporate-wide training. *Personnel Psychology* 50: 91-119.

National Center on the Educational Quality of the Workforce. 1995. *The other shoe: Education's contribution to the productivity of establishments. Catalog No. RE02. p. 2.*

Phillips, Jack J. 1991. *Handbook of training evaluation and measurement methods.* 3d ed. Houston, TX: Gulf Publishing.

———. 1994. *Measuring return on investment.* Alexandria, VA: American Society for Training and Development.

———. 1997. *Return on investment in training and performance improvement programs.* Houston, TX: Gulf Publishing.

8

Case Study: Manufacturing Performance

Suggestions for Using this Case Study

The case study below is based on an actual implementation of the performance improvement strategies described in this book. While details have been changed somewhat, this case is a "real-life example" of the system described in earlier chapters for setting goals, analyzing gaps, selecting appropriate performance solutions, and evaluating their results.

You can choose to read straight through the case or to use it as a learning exercise. If you'd like to practice applying the approach in the book, you can do so as you read. Stop periodically at the sections titled "Note to Readers" and ask yourself what you should do next. Before you read the next section, make your own plan based on the advice in previous chapters. Then read on to check your own approach against the decisions made by the consultants who worked the case. For example, when you read the section on focus group results, take a minute to categorize the problems you see mentioned by focus group members. Make a plan for how you would check the validity of the claims made during the focus group interviews. Then read on to compare your decisions to those actually made by the consultants. When you read the section on validating the causes of gaps, write a description of how you would solve each validated cause. Then describe the research-tested active ingredients necessary to bridge the gap based on your reading of this book and your own expertise. Make a plan for measuring the results of your solution at all four levels.

The Case

As a performance improvement consultant, you have been hired by QuickDisk, Inc., a company that manufactures and sells hard drives for PCs and other memory products. QuickDisk's assembly division has recently experienced a significant increase in damaged hard drives and a decrease in productivity. The frame assembly process was changed recently, and everyone thought that the changes had been very effective until production data suggested otherwise. Your client suggests that the assembly staff needs training in how to better handle components of the new process and a more efficient assembly method that will increase the number of units.

As you begin to discuss the problem with your client in more detail, you learn the following:

- When the new process was introduced a number of months ago, it was demonstrated to the assembly workers, but no formal training was provided.

- Damage to hard drive units has increased 32 percent in the past month alone (for a total of 41 percent above the expected damage rate established shortly after the new process was introduced).

- Unit productivity in the assembly group has fallen by 18 percent (for a total of 24 percent below the highest rate of productivity with the new process).

- On-time delivery to customers has decreased 38 percent. The company risks the loss of important customers, and the financial consequences could be disastrous.

Customers and assembly team members are very unhappy about the problem. Your client tells you that the assembly division must quickly raise its productivity levels in order to achieve the division's goals and make its contribution to the company's overall business goals and bottom line. The CFO tells you that if the problem continues, the company will lose significant market share for the current generation of drives, a serious blow to the company.

NOTE TO READERS:

Summarize the goals that you've been given by your client. Focus on the quantitative goals and be clear about the criteria for judging the achievement of qualitative goals. Then indicate how you will measure each goal.

In summary, QuickDisk's performance goals are as follows:

- Return the assembly group to its previous defect levels by eliminating all of the errors that have cropped up in the past few weeks. Maintain the change for at least six months until it is stable. That translates into a 41 percent decrease in errors over the start of this fiscal year.

- Return the assembly group to its previous productivity levels and maintain the change. That translates into a 24 percent increase in productivity.

- Restore the 38 percent loss in on-time delivery to customers and maintain it for at least six months.

Gap Analysis

This organization collects careful records of most stages in the manufacturing and delivery processes, including the number of frames produced each day, error rates (derived from quality checks), order and delivery cycle time, and the productivity of different teams in the cycles. The decision was made to use the existing database since, by all indications, it was reliable and accurate. The manufacturing records of the organization validate the estimates of the problem and the situation just before and after the change in the process.

You get permission to convene a focus group made up of various line employees in the assembly process. Line managers in the assembly area ask to sit in on the focus group or to hear recordings of the sessions. You get the support of your client to refuse this request because it might intimidate the assembly staff. Your request for closed meetings and confidential reporting is approved.

When the group meets, you give a brief history of the problem and ask open-ended questions about their views of the cause. A good bit of the subsequent discussion focuses on a description of what happens during the assembly process, but you do manage to learn the following:

- The frame assembly process had been changed six months before to a system that required the use of a reusable support. The supports quickly and significantly reduced assembly damage.

- The supports were initially greeted with enthusiasm by everyone as productivity increased, but after about three months, assembly teams gradually stopped using them consistently and productivity declined.

- Two members of your focus group remarked that the supports were inadequate and that they slowed down the assembly process because they were poorly designed.

- Two people remarked that they couldn't always locate a support when they needed one and that it was difficult to go back and forth between assembling with and without a support. When you followed up with the rest of the group about availability, they seemed to agree that supports were not always available when needed.

- Three people criticized the assembly setting as messy and disorganized, but none of the three could connect the assembly problem with the disorganization.

- One person felt that there was no problem with the process except that some people did not like the new approach because it was too difficult to use. You noticed that some heads nodded when the person made this comment. No one was willing to provide details, and you felt that their reluctance might be due to a fear of retribution from co-workers or line managers.

- Two people, including one supervisor in a line manager's focus group, felt that the problems were normal bugs that would resolve themselves as the system became more familiar to everyone.

Organizational Culture Profile

This organization is made up of a variety of national cultures and has been functioning for about nineteen years. You locate three managers who appear to be able to step back from the situation and describe the culture with some objectivity. You interview each of them separately in relaxed settings. You ask open-ended questions about a number of cultural issues, including how people in this setting make decisions, solve problems, handle feedback, and what they accept as reasons to adopt different ways to solve problems. From your interviews, you learn the following:

- Most people in the organization tend to make decisions and solve problems informally, in private, and prior to meetings where the decisions are to be discussed. Two of the three people you interviewed told stories about attending important meetings as new employees and being asked their views on problems, only to find that nearly everyone else in the meeting already shared one view about problems and solutions. Both people said that they felt like real outsiders until they caught on to the pattern. The third person had come from a similar organization and did not notice the pattern.

● All three told you, in different ways, that this organization handled performance feedback in very indirect, face-saving, and private ways. All expressed great frustration in their initial efforts to read what people were saying about performance. They also noticed that whenever anyone violated the unwritten rule that you do not criticize anyone, anywhere, anytime, the person who was criticized would react very defensively.

● When you asked what most people in the organization felt was a reason for changing some pattern or adopting a new approach, two out of the three people suggested that appearances were more important than reality. The third person suggested that this organization prized social acceptance, cooperation, and positive attitude. This appears to be a "We" culture.

NOTE TO READERS:
Make a preliminary list of your presumed causes of the performance gap. Then go on to the next section and check your ideas against the gap analysis of the performance consultant in the case.

Presumed Causes of Gaps

1. The lack of a formal training program might be a cause of the increased defects and decreased productivity, as your client believes. However, the supports were used successfully in the first few months with significant error reduction and productivity increases. Therefore, this is most likely not a *knowledge or skill* problem. The evidence points to a *process* or *materials* and/or a *motivational* problem.

2. The design or functioning of the new supports might cause the problem. The comments about their inadequacy and belief that they slowed the assembly process indicate this. The initial increase in productivity, however, is strong counterevidence to these suggested causes. Check the accuracy of the initial productivity increases to make certain that they are accurate. All new processes require familiarization time, so it is very impressive that productivity gains were evident almost from the beginning.

3. We need to investigate the suggestion by one person that the supports might not always be available. Determine if the support delivery and availability system is, in fact, working adequately since this *material resource* availability problem could be serious.

4. The comments about the messy and disorganized work environment might be best validated with an anonymous questionnaire, but only if other causes do not pan out. The three people who mentioned this problem could not connect it to the assembly problem, yet it might influence motivation (*buy-in, value*).

5. The agreement about the difficulty of the new process may indicate *under-confidence* on the part of some of the assembly team members. This might contribute to a persistence problem where people refuse to use the frames. This should be pursued in individual interviews with the people who made the complaint.

NOTE TO READERS:

Prioritize these presumed causes so that you can check out and validate each one. Make certain that it is a real problem and not someone's excuse or a mistaken perception. Look at the list above and prioritize them. Then look below and check the decisions made by the consultant.

Prioritization of Cause Validations

Beginning with the least disruptive and expensive to investigate:

A. The simplest cause to check is the trend line for defects and productivity following the introduction of the new frame assembly process. This will shed light on the question of training, as well as the suitability of the new process (1 and 2).

B. Next, check on the availability of the supports during the assembly process (3).

C. Next, check on any changes in work conditions, incentives, policy, or procedures that might have altered either the availability or the incentive to use the supports after they were introduced (1 and 3).

D. Check on the motivation of the assembly staff to determine whether a lack of confidence might be causing part of the problem (5).

If all of the above fail to identify a root cause, investigate the possibility that disorganization of the work environment is a cause (4). If not, restart the process.

Validation Results

A. Your client assures you that the problem does exist and is very serious. You checked work records indicating that performance moved to higher levels following the introduction of the new frame assembly process and then declined. This indicates that this is not a knowledge or skill problem, nor is it a materials flaw in the new frames.

B. You are surprised to discover when you check with purchasing and receiving that the supports are not consistently available for use during the assembly. You check further and learn that the assembly manager knows that the supplier of the supports has a production problem. Since the manager and the supplier have worked together on many past projects, the manager decided to tolerate the supply problem until it could be solved. This is a clear material resource cause of the gap.

C. The more you investigate, the more it appears that the drop in supply occurred just before productivity began to decline. As you investigate further, it becomes obvious that the manager in charge may not have received (or did not bother to check) information about the productivity drop for many weeks. Since the increase in productivity had been so dramatic and quick, most people thought that it would be durable. This may indicate a work process problem (the process of vendor selection and monitoring).

D. As you talk to employees, it is clear that they did not get feedback about the extent of the support supply problem. Instead, a couple of them who complained to the line manager were told that the problem was a "minor glitch" and that the real problem was due to lagging performance and resistance caused by a lack of training. They were told to do it the way they did it before the supports, until the supply problem was solved. These people apparently told the other assembly team members that they would all get training in the use of the supports. This apparently led to the comments about the difficulty of the process during the focus group meetings. This may have contributed to an under-confidence problem and a lack of trust for the line manager. Nothing else with regard to work conditions, incentives, policy, or procedures appears to have changed in this time period.

Validated Causes of Gaps

- Supports were not available for assembly work. Therefore, the new productivity was lost. Furthermore, the sporadic availability of the supports meant having to switch back and forth between the new methods and the old methods, causing further problems in set-up time and confusion (material resources, as well as process and procedures).

- No accurate feedback to assemblers about the support supply problem (information, trust).

- An ambiguous/irrational process was used for ordering supports. People were told to overcome a temporary lack of supports by doing it the old way until the "glitch" in supply fixed itself (material resources problem).

- Agreement among interviewees about the difficulty of using the supports suggests a possible under-confidence problem. Workers were told that they would get training to use the supports, which led the assembly workers to assume that they were using them incorrectly. This undermined their confidence and led them to assume that the process was more difficult than they expected.

> **NOTE TO READERS:**
>
> *Practice making recommendations based on the causes that were validated. Now that you know what is causing the gap, draw on the information in the previous chapters. First, identify the active ingredients of knowledge, skill, motivation, and work process research that will fix the validated causes of performance gaps. Second, think about how to translate those active ingredients for the culture of this organization and the problems they must solve (and who must solve them). Finally, integrate the active ingredients and the programs that you think will present them in the most effective ways for your clients and describe how you will measure results.*

Recommended Solutions

- Fix the support supply problem. Change the process of selecting vendors for critical supplies so that more than one vendor is qualified and available for all essential supplies and equipment.

- Clearly demonstrate the risks associated with disguising supply problems for any important supplies or tools and the benefits of admitting supply problems (modify manager overconfidence that led to the cover up).

- Insist that supervisors provide workers with correct and consistent information about assembly problems (improve feedback, increase trust, give accurate information).

- Inform the assembly teams that the production problem was caused by line management errors that caused a lack of supply, NOT by lack of knowledge and skill of assemblers (increase confidence, trust).

- Create confidence for teams by reminding the assemblers of their productivity increases in the beginning. Not only will this reduce under-confidence, but it will also counter the belief that the supports are badly designed and inefficient. This will create buy-in so that they are willing to give the frames another try.

- Use an anonymous survey to validate general agreement on messiness of the workplace. If validated, then clean up the workplace to make it a more pleasant place to work and to increase the value of assemblers for their work and workplace.

Actual Solutions

The division manager responsible for covering up his friend's supply problems and blaming the resulting frame assembly mistakes on the assembly teams was fired. The vice president visited the frame assembly teams to announce her decision to fire the manager and publicly apologized to them for the mess. She also announced a new policy that would require back-up supply plans for all critical equipment and materials. She promised that line managers would henceforth give the teams both accurate and timely information about production issues that were relevant to their job and invited them to communicate directly with her if they found an exception to that rule. She asked for a climate of trust and openness. She announced a new empowerment plan whereby line managers would collaborate with assembly teams to identify and solve production problems as they occurred. She also announced a new redecorating of their work space and asked them to repeat their extraordinary feat of eliminating assembly errors, since they now would have adequate supports and the system problems had been fixed. A long-term evaluation of results indicated that assembly errors fell off even lower than before, and productivity grew beyond the goal set for the project. These gains were holding three months after the problem was solved, and all but one of the customers lost as a result of the problem were placing new orders.

QuickDisk Performance Goals	Three-Month Results
Reduce errors by 41 percent to pre-problem levels.	Errors reduced 43 percent.
Increase productivity by 24 percent.	Productivity increased 31 percent.
Increase delivery time by 38 percent.	Deliveries increased by 46 percent.

In this case, the performance improvement consultants remarked that, at the three-month check, the workers "were transformed and totally motivated." Treating this problem as a motivational and materials supply/work process issue and addressing assembly workers respectfully paid huge dividends. The CFO estimated that the cost of the problem had reached about $4.5 million at the time it started to turn around. The cost of the intervention (including consulting time and all salary-replacement costs of staff who had any part in the solution) was about $287,000 and required about four weeks to diagnose the problem and design the solution.

9

Case Study:
Customer Service

Suggestions for Using this Case Study

The case study below is based on an actual implementation of the performance improvement strategies described in this book. While details have been changed somewhat, this case is a "real-life example" of the system described in earlier chapters for setting goals, analyzing gaps, selecting appropriate performance solutions, and evaluating their results.

You can choose to read straight through the case or to use it as a learning exercise. If you'd like to practice applying the approach in the book, you can do so as you read. Stop periodically at the sections titled "Note to Readers" and ask yourself what you should do next. Before you read the next section, make your own plan based on the advice in previous chapters. Then read on to check your own approach against the decisions made by the consultants who worked the case. For example, when you read the section on focus group results, take a minute to categorize the problems you see mentioned by focus group members. Make a plan for how you would check the validity of the claims made during the focus group interviews. Then read on to compare your decisions to those actually made by the consultants. When you read the section on validating the causes of gaps, write a description of how you would solve each validated cause. Then describe the research-tested active ingredients necessary to bridge the gap based on your reading of this book and your own expertise. Make a plan for measuring the results of your solution at all four levels.

The Case

In a meeting with your internal client, you learn that the customer service department has been targeted for major performance improvement. The upcoming introduction of new product lines is expected to increase the demand on customer service. Product success will depend, in large part, on customer satisfaction with the handling of service requests. Your objective is to significantly increase external customer satisfaction in preparation for the new product rollout.

Before you were called in, however, the area vice president had already requested a "state-of-the-art" system to ensure the customer service department could accomplish that goal. The urgent need for the system and the interest from upper management resulted in a speedy and impulsive selection of an outside vendor and implementation of a new approach.

This program has, predictably, gone bad—so bad, in fact, that the situation is now worse than when the program began. You have been called into a problem that is festering and about to get out of hand. You were not consulted when the program was chosen but are being asked to fix it. Your first effort is to discover what goals existed for the program. You determine that the quickly executed performance needs analysis resulted in the following customer service representative (CSR) performance goals:

CSR Performance Goals	Current Performance
Handle all customer requests in a one-call time frame.	Currently, 2.3 calls are required. (This is a 20 percent increase over the situation that existed when the program began.)
Have the power to make on-the-spot decisions to suspend or change service policy constraints in order to more adequately support customer needs and demands.	Currently, an average of 46 minutes is required to get agreement from various departments to handle customer requests, in addition to the average call time of 7 minutes. (There has been no change since the program began).
Deal more effectively with angry or frustrated customers. Reduce dissatisfied customer surveys to 20 percent (industry leader average).	Currently, 36 percent of customers surveyed after CSR calls indicated that they were "angry" or "very angry" at the way they had been treated (up from 31 percent when the program began).
Provide a level of service so that 70 percent customers are "satisfied" or "very satisfied" with their service interaction with the CSRs.	The level now is 45 percent (down from 58 percent when the new program began).

NOTE TO READERS:

Summarize the goals that you've been given by your client. Focus on the quantitative goals and be clear about the criteria for judging the achievement of qualitative goals. Then indicate how you will measure each goal.

In summary, the customer service department has the following performance goals:

- Decrease the number of customer calls required to handle requests from 2.3 to 1.

- Reduce time to handle a customer request from 53 total minutes to 7.

- Reduce the percentage of customers who are "angry" or "very angry" to 20 percent.

- Increase number of "satisfied" or "very satisfied" customers to 70 percent.

The new software for monitoring customer service calls contained features that measured the time per call, the number of calls required to complete a transaction, and the reaction of both CSRs and customers. It was decided to use the data collection features of the software to evaluate reaction to the new program, its impact, and transfer. The VP did not want to measure the bottom line impact until the program result at the first three levels was established.

Gap Analysis

The initial program included modifying policies and procedures to permit one-stop customer service. All CSRs were trained in the operation of the new customer service system and in active listening techniques to deal with angry or emotional customers. All CSRs were told that they could decide when to suspend or modify the company service policy in order to satisfy customer demands.

It is fortunate that the CSR call-monitoring software allows you to collect solid evaluation data for review as part of gap analysis. After the training, CSR phone interaction with customers was monitored, and a large number of customers took surveys administered by the software immediately after their interactions with a CSR. In addition, a random sample of customers were interviewed periodically for three months to ensure that their problem was handled.

You have also arranged to conduct a number of focus groups with both CSRs and customers. The moment the CSR focus groups enter the room where the interviews are being held, it is apparent that they are very emotional. After initial open-ended questions, it is clear that they are very angry at the results of the customer survey.

You learn the following from the CSR focus groups:

- Many complained that their managers were upset at the one-stop and "bend the rules" policies in the new program. While they did not suggest that the managers were actively discouraging their implementation of the program, many noted that more than one manager had described the new program in very negative terms. One outspoken manager was reported to have compared the program's implementation to "shooting ourselves in the collective foot in order to move forward." Another manager was widely quoted as having suggested that the company was "giving away the farm" to customers and that CSRs were now being told to "give customers anything they want." One CSR suggested that managers were "saluting the flag in public but trying to kill the program in private," because the program crossed lines of control and responsibility.

- Three CSRs mentioned that they had been complimented by their managers for holding the line on customers' demands when they had politely refused out of line requests by angry customers. None could remember compliments received for implementing the entire program effectively.

- One CSR noted that he had so many minor administrative tasks to perform in the service of the new program that he did not have time to help customers adequately. He also noted that most CSRs have no time to compare notes or learn from each other, and are forced to work alone.

- A number of CSRs expressed extreme discomfort with the active listening approach they had been taught for handling angry customers. They gave the impression that they were not able to make it work and offered the impression that other CSRs were having similar problems. Some traced their problems to a lack of understanding, and others seemed not to agree with the approach.

- Two of the CSRs thought the program was working very well and had heard no criticism of the new initiative or their own implementation of the program.

What you learned from the customer focus group:

- The majority of customers in your focus groups were angry and complained about the following:

  - CSRs were cranky and unsympathetic.

  - CSRs did not follow up as promised (nearly all had a problem here).

  - CSRs were insulting (one customer was upset when a CSR laughed and told him he was being too emotional about a problem).

  - A fix did not work, and they had to start the process over again with a different CSR.

  - CSRs seemed to be trying to get rid of the customer quickly rather than help them.

- One customer was totally delighted with her experience. A complex problem was solved very quickly on the telephone by a "polite and very concerned" CSR.

Organizational Culture Profile

This organization is made up of a variety of national cultures and it has been functioning for about thirteen years. You locate three managers who appear to be able to step back from the setting and describe the culture with some objectivity. You interview each of them separately in relaxed settings. You ask open questions about a number of cultural issues including how people make decisions, solve problems, handle feedback, and what they accept as reasons to adopting different ways to solve problems. You learn the following from your interviews:

- Most people in the organization tend to make decisions and solve problems formally, attending meetings in which an effort is made to achieve consensus. Two of the three people you interviewed said that this pattern had caused them a considerable amount of trouble when they were first hired. Both told stories about attending important meetings as new employees and being asked their views on problems, only to find that nearly everyone else in the meeting was trying to find an approach that others could accept. One said, "We go to great lengths not to disagree, and we value flexibility and complete consensus." One said that she thought she had been hired by "an organism rather than an organization. It was as if no action could be taken unless every part of the organism agreed on direction and mode of attack." The third person had come from a similar organization and did not notice the pattern. This seems to have earmarks of a "We" culture.

- All three told you, in different ways, that this organization handled performance feedback in very indirect but candid ways. "Generally we tell each other what we think, emphasizing the positive and softening the blows on the negative stuff so that we do not hurt each other too much." All expressed great frustration in their initial efforts to "read what people were saying" about performance. They also noticed that the reaction to even private criticism tended to be very defensive.

- When you asked what most people in the organization felt was a reason for changing some pattern or adopting a new approach, two of the three people suggested that, as one put it, "not making a mistake is more important than succeeding at a more positive goal." The third person suggested that this organization prized detail work and following rules. "We tend to be perfectionists," she said, "and we are proud of it."

Presumed Causes of Gaps

1. The obvious problem to explore here is the *buy-in* difficulty caused by negative reactions of managers reported to be resisting the program. Check to see if managers are supporting the program. At the very least, many CSRs believe that managers are resisting, and beliefs may be impacting implementation of the program. Serious attention needs to be devoted to investigating this possible cause.

2. It is possible that there is a *knowledge and skill* problem—or also perhaps a *transfer* problem—with the active listening techniques for working with angry customers. A number of CSRs indicated that they were having problems with the approach, and customer comments mirror this problem. Customer complaints about CSR ridicule should not happen if the technique is being used successfully. Check to make sure CSRs are able to use this approach.

3. Check to see why the real-time monitoring of CSR telephone conversations did not catch these problems before they got out of hand. Who was monitoring the calls? What were the results of that monitoring activity? This *feedback and information* issue might have hidden the problem until it was too late.

4. CSRs might have too much paperwork and administrative tasks preventing them from consulting with their customer service colleagues. *Work goals* may need to be prioritized or clarified. It is also possible that not enough time is allotted for handling individual customer calls. A number of customers complained that CSRs were not taking enough time to handle their problems. These are potential *goal and priority* problems. The complaints should be checked out.

5. Overall, one suspects a *confidence* problem exists for both mangers (*overconfidence*) and some CSRs (*under-confidence*). In addition, the managers' public criticism of the new plan may be undermining the CSRs' buy-in and, therefore, their *motivation* to use the system and persist at it when they encounter any problems.

> **NOTE TO READERS:**
> *Prioritize these presumed causes so that you can check out and validate each one. Make certain that it is a real problem and not someone's excuse or a mistaken perception. Look at the list above and prioritize them. Then look below and check the decisions made by the consultant.*

Prioritization of Cause Validations

Beginning with the least disruptive and expensive to investigate:

A. Review the time limit on CSR calls to see if it is adequate to perform required tasks. See if the various tasks that must be handled by the CSRs have been prioritized. Then check to see if the CSRs are aware of the priorities and have been following them (4).

B. Check the software that permits monitoring of CSR calls to see if these features are available and functioning. If they are available and working, check the software records to see if they were used by the managers to monitor calls (3).

C. Ask a sample of CSRs to demonstrate the active listening technique to see if they can use it correctly. Check the CSRs' confidence levels for using the active listening technique and other features of the new program (2 and 5).

D. Use outside consultants to interview managers individually (and protect their identity to ensure candid replies) to learn whether they are rejecting the new program. Check work records to see whether they have been making decisions and taking actions that support all features of the program (1 and 5).

Validation Results

The results of your validation are:

A. In your investigation of the administrative tasks faced by the CSRs, you conclude that the time criticism may be valid. The problem, however, is most likely not due to administrative tasks, but instead to the amount of average time allotted to each call. The CSRs find the time limits very punishing, and the issue may be damaging their buy-in for the approach. The new system should consider permitting a higher average telephone contact time than was originally anticipated. This issue should be subjected to a separate study to determine an average time allotment that is adequate but efficient. At this point, the limited call time is damaging the buy-in from CSRs for the new system. They need motivational support that is similar to the managers.

B. You were surprised to find that, during the early stages of the program, the telephone calls were generally not monitored. This task had been assigned to line managers, and many of those managers were resisting the implementation. Those responsible pointed to a glitch in the monitoring software. However, there was no record that those responsible had attempted to fix what may have been a convenient problem. Check to see if the program was adequate to perform the job (if not, then you have a material resources problem). If the program does have all the necessary components, then the problem is the buy-in from managers.

C. When you checked on the CSRs' knowledge about the active listening technique for dealing with angry customers, you found that they seemed to know how to use the technique, but were not doing so. This would suggest a buy-in and a transfer problem, rather than a knowledge and skill or a confidence problem. You conclude that they may not be using the technique because of manager resistance. When the resistance is reduced, the use of the technique may increase. It is not clear how much manager buy-in affects the average CSR. For those CSRs with lower confidence, at least, management resistance does seem to make the task more difficult.

D. After a number of interviews and anonymous surveys, you conclude that a significant core of managers in a variety of departments are very angry about the new CSR program. Most of these managers are passively hostile. They are not actively resisting but are making negative comments in contexts where they will be overheard. These comments are quickly communicated to many of the CSRs, who believe that if they fully implement the new program they will be punished. It is also obvious that the organization invested a great deal of effort training the CSRs for the new program, but did not invest enough effort to secure buy-in from managers. Many managers seem to fear a loss of influence and resent the territorial conflicts fostered by the new program. Research in this area strongly indicates that any fix must include utility elements that are valued by the managers to get their buy-in. They must be convinced that the new program will make them more, not less, effective.

Validated Causes of Gaps

- Managers are definitely angry, making negative remarks where they would be overheard (lack of buy-in, overconfidence).

- CSRs do fear being punished for actively implementing the program as intended (buy-in).

- CSRs are convinced that the additional administrative tasks reduce the time required to address other company needs, as well as time for sharing war stories and solutions with colleagues as they had been advised to do (goals, priorities). Time is too limited for expanded customer service. The average time needed to expand customer service (not just system administration tasks) should be renegotiated after thorough study.

- CSRs are uncomfortable with the active listening procedure. Some say they do not understand it (buy-in and knowledge and skills). Some CSRs with lower confidence levels believe that their managers are making their task impossible (under-confidence).

- Customers complained that CSRs were arbitrary and unsympathetic or insulting (active listening buy-in failure) and that they tried to get rid of customers as quickly as possible (active listening buy-in failure and/or inadequate average call time constraints).

- Calls weren't being monitored by managers (buy-in problem by managers and/or material resource problem with software).

NOTE TO READERS:

Practice making recommendations based on the causes that were validated. Now that you know what is causing the gap, draw on the information in the previous chapters. First, identify the active ingredients of knowledge, skill, motivation, and work process research that will fix the validated causes of performance gaps. Second, think about how to translate those active ingredients for the culture of this organization and the problems they must solve (and who must solve them). Third, integrate the active ingredients and the programs that you think will present them in the most effective ways for your clients and describe how you will measure results.

Recommended Solutions

- Fix the lack of managerial support by getting the managers' buy-in to support the solution.

- Give CSRs some say in how to revise the system to increase their buy-in.

- Set up an effective system to help monitor calls.

- Increase the expected average time CSRs should spend on a call so that they can adequately deal with the customers' problems. CSRs should also have time to address company coordination needs and share solutions with colleagues to increase the effectiveness of the system. In order to do this, it might be necessary to hire and train more CSRs.

- Get CSR buy-in to use active listening approach to handle upset customers.

- Monitor whether CSRs with lower confidence levels change their behavior when/if their managers change their attitude.

Actual Solutions

The vice president's arbitrary decision to implement this program in an organization where consensus was an important part of the culture was identified as the primary cause of this problem. An outside consultant was given the unwelcome task of giving the VP this feedback. The consultant explained that the result of a failure to get manager buy-in was a serious loss of confidence by CSRs who did not use the new system with customers. Their anger and resentment was communicated to customers who reacted with even more frustration and anger than before the problem began. The VP was advised that, in the future, he must either work to change the organization's culture so that people more easily accept and implement top-down decisions, or else get buy-in for new work processes or policies that require big changes in current operating processes.

The VP was asked to talk to the managers and the CSRs and take responsibility for the problem. He was not happy about it, but he did the right thing and went even further. He promised to include the managers in all future decisions that would influence their areas, and he made a similar promise to the CSRs.

The performance support staff was given the job of fixing the system and making it work. Since the organizational culture led people to expect to be consulted, they asked managers and CSRs to appoint "fix-it" committees. The committees planned the re-implementation of the active listening strategy to improve customer reactions during calls. They also studied the necessary average call time for CSRs to adequately handle customer needs (the CFO of the organization was consulted and sent a representative to help steer this process so that it was cost-effective). Finally, the managers worked out an acceptable system for handling cross-unit policy so that CSRs could implement unit policies without having to constantly consult the units themselves.

The result of the committees' work is that the CSRs began transferring and using the active listening approach, and they fully implemented a revised one-call system. The managers fully supported the new system with both formal and informal positive feedback to the CSRs and with helpful monitoring of their customer calls. Evidence from the CSR monitoring software indicated after three months that goals were on track.

CSR Performance Goals	Three-Month Results
Decrease calls required to handle requests from 2.3 to 1.	Call handling reduced to 1.6.
Reduce call time from 53 minutes to 7 minutes.	Time reduced to 18 minutes.
Reduce angry customers to 20 percent.	Angry replies reduced to 24 percent.
Increase "satisfied" to 70 percent.	"Satisfied" increased to 67 percent.

Since no baseline measure of the cost and benefit of the previous system was made at the beginning of the project, it was not possible to accurately estimate the impact of the project on the bottom line. The CFO representative estimated that the financial benefit to the company of the revised program was about 400 times its total cost (including the salary cost of everyone engaged in the program while they fixed the problem).

10

Case Study:
Sales Performance

Suggestions for Using this Case Study

The case study below is based on an actual implementation of the performance improvement strategies described in this book. While details have been changed somewhat, this case is a "real-life example" of the system described in earlier chapters for setting goals, analyzing gaps, selecting appropriate performance solutions, and evaluating their results.

You can choose to read straight through the case or to use it as a learning exercise. If you'd like to practice applying the approach in the book, you can do so as you read. Stop periodically at the sections titled "Note to Readers" and ask yourself what you should do next. Before you read the next section, make your own plan based on the advice in previous chapters. Then read on to check your own approach against the decisions made by the consultants who worked the case. For example, when you read the section on focus group results, take a minute to categorize the problems you see mentioned by focus group members. Make a plan for how you would check the validity of the claims made during the focus group interviews. Then read on to compare your decisions to those actually made by the consultants. When you read the section on validating the causes of gaps, write a description of how you would solve each validated cause. Then describe the research-tested active ingredients necessary to bridge the gap based on your reading of this book and your own expertise. Make a plan for measuring the results of your solution at all four levels.

The Case

In a conversation with your sponsor, the executive vice president of Crain Properties, a large commercial realty and construction company, you learn that a recent attempt to change their approach to property sales and leasing has gone off course. About eight months ago, after a serious dip in company income, management decided to shake up the sales department by introducing a revised sales strategy. This new strategy was based on cognitive theories on customer motivation and included a new approach to direct selling and a wider integrated team approach that incorporated sales, legal, marketing, and maintenance staff.

Your sponsor believes the sales staff has resisted attempts to change their approach. During the years when sales and rentals met and exceeded expectations, the sales staff were encouraged to "do their own thing." A year of less than ideal results led to the identification of an approach that should have solved the problem. It was adopted, and everyone was trained to use it. Yet sales have fallen by 31 percent and leasing is off 26 percent from levels at the time when the new approach was planned.

The new approach did not seek to replace all aspects of the older sales approach (as one manager put it, "they tried not to throw out the baby with the bath water"). Yet it did require sales to adopt new methods for overcoming customer resistance and for identifying, contacting, and attracting new customers for sales and leasing. It also required more collaboration, with salespeople assigned to teams made up of representatives from marketing, legal, and maintenance. When the approach was introduced, there seemed to be widespread relief and acceptance. The head of sales was widely quoted as saying that she had "asked for this a year ago."

The organization has been using the new approach for four months, and first quarter results have been dismal. Sales and rentals have actually decreased slightly over the average of the previous two quarters before the program began. Since the high water mark in sales and leasing was achieved a year before the program began, sales are now down 40 percent and leasing is now down 50 percent from that high. Equally damaging is the fact that no new customers have been added.

The VP tells you that problems with the new system started almost from the beginning. While the marketing, legal, and maintenance staff were enthusiastic or positive, the established sales staff was heard to voice private objections to parts of the approach. This was expected—high performers in sales in this organization tend to be very independent-minded. The only other early problem was that a few legal staff members thought that their involvement was adding more work to their already full schedules. The team who managed the change, including the training for the new approach, attempted to meet the objections of the top performers in sales. As a result, they thought that everyone was on board as the new approach was rolled out.

When company accounting data was checked, it is clear that sales and leasing operations experienced a dip approximately twenty months ago. Your client wants to get back to the high water mark and has asked you to set the goal of achieving the income level that matches pre-dip levels. He also wants sales and marketing to focus on drawing in 20 percent new customers. Thus, the gap you are trying to close is the difference between current sales and leasing income and the business goal of achieving the income levels achieved twenty months prior to the beginning of the new sales approach, as well as adding 20 percent new customers for sales and leasing.

> **NOTE TO READERS:**
> *Summarize the goals that you've been given by your client. Focus on the quantitative goals and be clear about the criteria for judging the achievement of qualitative goals. Then indicate how you will measure each goal.*

In summary, Crain Properties' goals are as follows:

- Increase sales by 40 percent to bring them back in line with previous highs.

- Increase leases by 50 percent to bring them back in line with previous highs.

- Increase new customers to 20 percent of customer base and retain existing customers.

- Increase staff use of new sales and leasing approach to 100 percent.

Gap Analysis

Crain records all sales, rentals, and new customer counts daily. A direct measure of new program use was captured using interviews with customers that were incorporated into the negotiation and signing of sales or lease contracts. A random sample of sales lead contacts was interviewed by phone on a random basis if the lead did not result in a sale or rental agreement. Legal, marketing, sales, and service staff were interviewed about the compliance of other departments (for example, sales people commented on the use of the system by legal, marketing, and service staff, but were not asked about sales staff).

You arrange for two focus groups—one made up of representatives from sales, production, and service and one composed entirely of sales representatives. From the sales, production, and service focus group, you learn the following:

- Sales representatives were upset about the new approach. All of the sales people had the same impression—"this approach is not working, and things are only going to get worse."

- Many sales people voiced the opinion that the dip in income was due to a softening of the market, not to a failure to adopt the new sales approach.

- Marketing representatives suggested that the market had not softened but that the potential customer base had shifted to new sectors.

- You noticed no indications that marketing, legal, or maintenance were having problems with the new sales program, even though there were rumors that some of the legal office might resist.

- A number of comments made by legal and marketing people suggested that sales staff might not be cooperating with other members of their cross-functional teams. One person said that sales acted as if team activities were a waste of time and went further to suggest that "many of the salespeople act like they are the entire show and we are along to take credit for their efforts."

- Many participants mentioned issues such as a lack of time to implement the approach, the lack of a database to allow them to track sales and leasing targets and events, and existing policies and procedures that made collaboration difficult.

From the focus group of sales representatives, you learn the following:

- The more experienced salespeople expressed the strong impression that they were doing fine and were using the new system, but suggested that "the market is soft, and no one wants to buy now."

- Two of the experienced people became quite difficult when you attempted to ask them for details about which parts of the new method they liked the best or found the most difficult. The general point of view was that the problem was weak demand, not a weak implementation of the new method.

- The younger and more recently hired sales staff seemed less certain of their performance with the new system. Some of the new hires suggested that the new system was "very difficult" to implement. When you asked them if they were able to get help from more experienced sales staff, the answer was ambiguous. You have the impression that they tried and failed to get help from some of their more successful colleagues.

You decide to develop a focus group for new and less experienced salespeople. You learn the following:

- Many of the more experienced staff were not using the new methods effectively. One of the newer salespeople complained that "these more established sales and leasing reps are doing what has always worked for them with some tweaks. It doesn't seem to me to be what we learned to do in training." Heads nodded when this statement was made. Yet your attempt to follow up and get details was met with a reluctance to elaborate.

- The new sales staff felt that they had no positive models to help them. Experienced staff seemed to be reluctant to mentor new people, and sales managers were over-committed with the problems caused by the dip in sales.

You arrange a mixed group of sales, marketing, and maintenance staff—but without any salespeople—and learn:

- Nearly everyone was upset at the lack of cooperation from experienced salespeople.

- The cross-functional teams were not working effectively because, in the view of these focus group members, sales was "uncooperative." A number of new work processes to link the groups more effectively were started by the teams, but they had hit a wall and couldn't achieve more without the full participation of sales.

Finally you decide to hold a focus group made up of very experienced sales staff and learn:

- In general, they were resentful at being asked to spend time in the focus group. "Ask the marketing people to give you honest answers to these questions," one suggested. "The problem is in marketing, not sales." They suggested that marketing had been "pressured" to say that the market was strong.

- They appeared resentful that you took their time to talk about the new sales method or ask them about sales problems. "The new method is not the problem, nor is it the solution," said one individual. "We know what we're doing in sales, if you could just invent new methods for the customers!"

Organizational Culture Profile

This organization is made up of a variety of national cultures and has been functioning for about thirty-three years. You locate three managers who appear to be able to describe the culture with some objectivity. All were recent hires and all had worked for a number of other organizations before they were hired. You interview each of them separately in relaxed settings. You ask open questions about a number of cultural issues including how people in this setting make decisions, solve problems, handle feedback, and what they accept as reasons to adopt different ways to solve problems. You learn the following:

- Most people tend to make decisions and solve problems formally, usually in meetings where an effort is made to achieve a democratic vote if there is disagreement. "We go to great lengths to find a majority in favor of a solution rather than to find the best solution" said one person. One person said that when first hired, she thought she had been captured by "a legislature rather than a business organization…. It was as if no vote could be taken unless a political campaign had been waged and the result of the vote known before it was held." The third person had come from a similar organization and did not notice the pattern.

- All three told you, in different ways, that this organization handled performance feedback in very direct and candid ways. "Everyone here knows where she or he stands, all the time." Yet all three mentioned that the feedback tended to focus on what was done well instead of on mistakes or inadequate efforts. All noted that the tendency was to "accent the positive" while not "eliminating the negative." They also noticed that the reaction to this feedback tended to be positive, accepting, and affirming and that most people in the organization were independently-minded and success-focused.

- Two out of three people suggested that "achieving business and performance goals is more important than avoiding mistakes." In general, they said that the organization tries to generate an environment where mistakes are okay, provided they are acknowledged and the staff tries to do better. "Succeeding at a positive goal is definitely more important than making mistakes as we pursue the goal." The third person suggested that this organization is "results-oriented, individualistic, and optimistic."

Presumed Causes of Gaps

1. Experienced sales and leasing reps are convinced the problem is not their implementation of the system, but the market. They resent having their competence questioned (*buy-in, overconfidence*).

2. Less experienced salespeople are trying hard but finding implementing the approach too difficult (*knowledge/skills*). They also lack mentoring and feedback support from both the sales managers, who are busy trying to fix the sales problem, and experienced salespeople, who are unwilling to share and teach.

3. Sales staff claim they lack time to fully implement the approach.

4. The electronic database to track sales targets and events may not be working (*material resources*).

5. Existing *policies and work processes* may make collaboration difficult.

Prioritization of Cause Validations

Beginning with the least disruptive and expensive to investigate:

A. Review the electronic database system and see if it is working (4).

B. Examine the job procedures to see if the available time for the sales staff to implement the approach is adequate (3).

C. Check to see if the experienced sales people are using the new approach and are contacting new customers from the areas identified by marketing (1).

D. Check to see if the sales staff knows how to perform the procedures for the new approach. Also check on whether sales managers and more experienced sales staff are mentoring the new staff (2).

E. Interview individual team members and observe team activities to see if there are serious barriers to the functioning of the cross-functional teams (5).

Validation Results

A. The database system is functioning properly. It is capable of reporting a great variety of internal data including: a) daily planned and completed sales contacts; b) completed sales by day, week and month; and c) comparisons with previous quarters. Sales people, however, are not using the new system. The system currently being used by most sales staff is an old chalkboard in one of the office spaces that is managed by a few senior salespeople. This is another extension of the *buy-in* problem; the new tracking system would replace the blackboard if the sales staff adopted the new sales method.

B. A review of job procedures does not indicate any problems preventing implementation of the new approach.

C. A thorough transfer evaluation indicates that very few of the sales staff are actually using the new method. The training staff who originally participated in the introduction of the new method help you with the evaluation. They report to you that the more experienced staff seem to have avoided using the new method altogether (though some have adopted a surface-level version which distracts from the fact that they are still using their familiar and established methods). When you tell the sales manager about your observation, she is shocked. She is certain that the experienced sales staff actually believe that they are using the method, or at lest the "best parts" of it. This indicates a *buy-in* problem that has prevented transfer of the knowledge and skills learned about the new approach in training. Marketing assures you that the market has been strong for the past five quarters—although the customer based has shifted to new sectors. Many of the organization's older customers are either not buying or are buying less. The new customers have been identified by the revised sales method. However, it seems likely that the sales staff are not taking advantage of the shift in the customer base. Instead they continue to contact old customers and are missing the market. This is an extension of the *buy-in* problem for the new method.

D. New sales staff are having trouble using the new methods, but they have bought in and seem to be investing a great deal of effort. Therefore, you conclude that their problem is a *lack of transfer support* on the job.

E. You cannot find any examples of policy or work processes that are preventing the use of the new method or the functioning of the work teams. Therefore, work processes are not part of the problem. The cross-functional teams are not collaborating as intended; they have become distracted with minor goals and are not pursuing their main objectives. The reason for this problem is that sales members on the teams are not collaborating.

Validated Causes of Gaps

- There is a serious problem with buy-in from experienced salespeople. They are not using the new approach or the new tracking system.

- Less experienced sales people have not received the necessary transfer support to be able to implement the new approach successfully.

- Cross-functional teams are not working effectively due to the sales staff's refusal to cooperate.

> **NOTE TO READERS:**
> *Practice making recommendations based on the causes that were validated. Now that you know what is causing the gap, draw on the information in the previous chapters. First, identify the active ingredients of knowledge, skill, motivation, and work process research that will fix the validated causes of performance gaps. Second, think about how to translate those active ingredients for the culture of this organization and the problems they must solve (and who must solve them). Thirdly, integrate the active ingredients and the programs that you think will present them in the most effective ways for your clients and describe how you will measure results.*

Recommended Solutions

- Get *buy-in* from experienced sales reps who are *overconfident* and have wrong beliefs about the market and are therefore resisting the new method and market data by:

- Showing them marketing data and challenging their beliefs about the market (*test*);

- Demonstrating the risks of avoiding the approach and incentives for using it (*utility value*);

- Challenging them to show their sales ability (*skill value*).

- Provide on-the-job coaching by experienced sales people for less experienced new hires—and more experienced staff who may not fully understand the new approach—to help them transfer what they learned in training to the job.

- Create *value* for the daily use of the electronic data base by all sales people.

- Ask sales manager to *monitor and coach* the difficult sales people.

Actual Solutions

The VP decided to take your advice to start by focusing exclusively on convincing the experienced sales people to accept marketing's claim that the market has been changed by a shift in their customer base. He agreed with your advice that challenging sales overconfidence by testing their mistaken belief in a soft market had to be the first step in overcoming their resistance. Since the organizational culture supported open discussion and decision-making, the VP and the head of sales worked together to hire an outside marketing consultant to produce a "more objective" marketing study. The VP wisely asked senior salespeople to agree to accept the results of the new study. This kind of test and acceptance of results is the active ingredient in all attempts to change the views of overconfident people who are resistant to a new approach. Three weeks later, the results of the study (and a comparison with the earlier internal marketing studies) were shared with sales in an open meeting. The two studies agreed completely on almost every point. The VP and sales manager resisted the temptation towards "we told you so" messages. They simply reminded the sales group of their earlier promise and challenged them to act on the results of the new study. They asked them to adopt the new approach, use the electronic data base to identify new customers, give coaching support to the new people, and give their best effort to make the teams successful. They set specific, challenging, week-by-week goals for new customer targets and asked them to retain existing customers. They clearly described the risk of not buying into the study results by suggesting that "now is the time to think about whether you want to stay on our team."

The VP and sales manager wanted to offer incentives based on team competition. You asked them to wait to implement competition for fear that the teams would work against each other in a destructive way. Eventually they agreed to start a quota incentive plan that rewarded sales and leasing representatives and their teams for achieving their quotas for new customers. In addition, senior staff members were assigned as coaches to new sales staff. The coach and trainee pairs were organized in such a way that trainees could remind the coach of the essentials of the new sales method and the coaches could suggest ways that the trainee could implement the method with new customers.

Finally, a more user-friendly interface for accessing the electronic database was designed to resemble a car dashboard. It gave clear indications of goal progress including, for example, the number of new customer contacts, daily and weekly sales, leasing results, and current customer retention data, and it permitted access to team and individual data including contact schedules.

A summary of the goals of this project and the results achieved three months after the incentive system was introduced appears below. It appears that the solution is working.

Sales Performance Goals	Three-Month Results
Increase new customers to 20 percent of base.	New customers 14 percent of base and growing.
Increase sales by 40 percent.	Sales up 28 percent—most with new customers.
Increase leases by 50 percent.	Leases up 31 percent—most with new customers.
Increase sales use of method to 100 percent.	Evidence that sales compliance is 90 percent +.
Maintain existing customer base level.	Drop of 2 percent in existing customers.

11

Postscript: Turning Research Into Results

IF YOU HAVE REACHED THIS POINT, you may be considering adopting some of the ideas you've read about. This final chapter distills the approach into a few main points and suggestions. Human performance research can be applied to a project of any size or scope, and the benefits of adopting a research-based system of performance improvement are plenty. If you have doubts, select a small project and apply a limited version of the approach as we have outlined here.

Determine your business goal and the related performance you want to improve. Quantify the gap between your current level and the desired future performance levels.

Be clear about the problem you want to solve before you consider any solution. Too many performance improvement projects do not begin with a clear analysis of the business reason for setting a new performance goal. Performance specialists are often simply told:

"We need an incentive program (or a training program, or a new business process)...."
When confronted with circumstances like these and a short timeframe for delivery,
adopt the 25/75 percent approach. Spend a quarter of the time you're allotted
analyzing whether that solution will actually achieve the goal(s) you want to
accomplish. The solution and the timeframe you were given probably do not reflect
much, if any, analysis of the problem. Unless you ask questions now, you're staking
your professional credibility on the solution presented. If you conclude later that the
timeline is unrealistic or the solution is wrong, your client is likely to perceive this
bad news as a gap in your performance, not in his or her request.

Ask about the impact chain that will occur if the suggested solution works. What
will the solution influence, and how will that influence connect with business goals?
Analyze the situation to see if the expectation is valid. Check to see what people are
doing (and not doing) to reach emphasized performance goals. Quantify the distance
between what people are doing and what they need to do . Once you accomplish this
early step, you can be confident that a problem exists and that solving it may produce
business results. If the problem does not exist (or you find a different problem), go
back and try to renegotiate the task you've been given. Offer to provide solid evidence
of increased performance. You may not be able to measure an actual increase in
business, but you can determine that some process that contributes to profits has
been improved. Most important is that you are now able to determine why the goal
has not already been achieved, fit the solution to the actual situation, and measure
results to ensure that you've achieved your goal. Worst case scenario would be for
you to determine that you do not need a solution (either because the problem will
solve itself if you leave it alone or because there is no problem to solve) or that a
different type of solution is required.

**Look for the causes of the gaps you've identified by using the
interview, focus group, and survey strategies described in
chapter 3.**

Be open to finding out things that you do not expect. You should only expect that the
gaps you have measured are caused (and can be solved) by knowledge and skills,
motivation, and/or organizational processes and materials. Note all suggestions. Look
for patterns. Validate the views that emerge by checking work records and other
organizational data. We find it valuable to write a description of the evidence for
each cause we identify.

Even when organizations are not experiencing performance problems, they can
benefit from increasing motivation, from more education to help key people deal

with future unexpected changes, and from improvements in organizational processes. These projects must be organized in the same way. Start by asking what types of knowledge, motivation, and organizational processes are necessary to achieve the new goals for everyone involved.

Once you know what type of solution you require, make a list of the research-tested "active ingredients" of performance improvement products that have a high probability of solving the problem.

Use the procedures and checklists presented in chapters 4, 5, and 6 to identify the active ingredients you must have to achieve performance goal targets. Once you have a list of the program components you need, use it as a shopping list to identify prospective products or services, or to design your own program. If necessary, check the current state of the research on any topic by accessing some of the resources we list at the end of these chapters.

It is important to build the various types of active ingredients you identify into an integrated performance program. For example, if you need a training program, improved work processes, and a quota-based incentive program, why not construct one integrated and coherent approach to providing all three interventions? Motivational issues can be addressed in a training program (and afterwards on the job), and new or improved work processes can be presented and practiced during training.

Develop a solid evaluation design for reactions, learning (or motivation), and transfer to the job. Cost-benefit evaluation is built into this approach if you estimate the cost and benefit of achieving the goal at the front end of the project.

Evaluation is the only way you'll learn about all four levels of impact. Solid evaluation can be built into all types of programs in ways that will be more or less invisible. For example, assessing reactions only requires a few brief questions at the end of the program or a program day. Evaluating learning during training, the motivational impact of programs, or the utility of new work processes can be accomplished by tracking participants' practice exercises. Cost-benefit analysis is the natural outcome of adding financial issues to the measurement of gaps at the start and the end of a program. Even if your organization does not require program evaluation, the strategies we suggest in chapter 7 will add undeniable proof to the argument that your program made the difference. Constant evaluation also serves as an early warning system because it alerts you to problems in time for you to make necessary revisions.

Use the human performance analysis process constantly so that you are detecting performance gaps as business conditions change.

An unexpected benefit of the successful trial of a research-based approach is that it can become the basis for continued performance improvement. All successful organizations need a process in place to constantly identify, analyze, and close performance gaps that are preventing business goals. Remember, performance improvement can be directed at future opportunities as well as current problems. In that case, the focus is on the gap between the level of performance today and an improved level of performance that will enable the organization to capitalize on a business opportunity. Since all organizations are unique, constant, iterative analysis of goals, gaps, and solutions ensures that performance improvement programs are tuned to fit your organizational culture. The front-end analysis, solution, and evaluation process yield important information about the organization and its employees, as well as business goal benefits. That increased self-knowledge adds significantly to the benefit achieved by increased employee performance.

As you begin to explore this approach to performance improvement, take advantage of the numerous published resources available to guide you in the design, implementation, and management of gap analysis activities. Many other writers have provided very detailed and useful plans for designing and conducting the front-end analysis and evaluation strategies we describe in this book. See, for example, the comprehensive handbook edited by Stolovitch and Keeps (1999); a socially responsible and research-based view of goal setting and front end analysis by Kaufman (2000); an excellent approach to gap analysis project management strategies by Fuller (1998); the clear and insightful suggestions made to those who manage this process by Bob Mager (1997) and by Rummler and Brache (1995); and an excellent series of suggestions by Fuller and Farrington (1999) about how to make the transition from training services to human performance management. We are also impressed with the new research-based design system for very complex knowledge recently described in an award winning book by van Merrienboer (1997; see also van Merrienboer, Clark, and de Croock 2002). We strongly recommend these authors and texts.

The unique benefit of this approach is in the use of gap analysis and in the active ingredients approach to selecting products and services. What you will not find in other published materials is a coherent approach to using research and evaluation results to select effective solutions to performance challenges. The approach in this book is the missing ingredient in human performance technology. Most performance specialists emphasize the front-end process of analyzing problems and opportunities, and the design, implementation, and evaluation of programs. Yet nearly all of the existing approaches lack any connection to the huge body of performance research available. There are many reasons why performance gaps exist, but there are no good reasons for the problem to continue—if you apply the strategies we suggest. Why not move towards the use of research-based findings? What can you lose, and how significant are the gains you can expect?

References

American Management Association (AMA). 1997. *Corporate job creation, job elimination and downsizing: Summary of key findings*. New York: American Management Association.

American Psychological Association (APA), American Educational Research Association (AERA), and National Council on Measurement in Education (NCME). 1985. *Standards for educational and psychological testing*. Washington, D.C.: American Psychological Association.

Anderson, John R. 1993. *Rules of the mind*. Englewood-Cliffs, NJ: Lawrence Erlbaum Associates.

Anderson, John R., and Christian J. Labiere. 1998. *The atomic components of thought*. Hillsdale, NJ: Lawrence Erlbaum Associates.

Anderson, John R., Lynne M. Reder, and Herbert A. Simon. 1996. Situated learning and education. *Educational Researcher* 25, no. 4: 5-11.

———. 1997. Situative versus cognitive perspectives: Form versus substance. *Educational Researcher* 26, no. 1: 18-21.

Axelrod, Elizabeth L., Helen Handfield-Jones, and Timothy A. Welsh. 2001. War for talent, part two. *The McKinsey Quarterly* 2.

Azar, Beth. 2000. Blinded by hindsight. *Monitor on Psychology* (May): 28-29.

Bandura, Albert. 1997. *Self-efficacy: The exercise of control*. New York: W.H. Freeman.

Baldwin, Tim T., and J. Kevin Ford. 1988. Transfer of training: A review and directions for future research. *Personnel Psychology* 41: 63-105.

Bargh, John A., and Tanya L. Chartrand. 1999. The unbearable automaticity of being. *American Psychologist* 54, no. 7: 462-479.

Barsalou, Lawrence W. 1992. *Cognitive psychology: An overview for cognitive scientists.* Hillsdale, NJ: Lawrence Erlbaum Associates.

Bechtell, Michele L. 1996. *The management compass: Steering the corporation using hoshin planning.* An American Management Association Management Briefing. New York: AMA Membership Publications Division.

Belasco, James A. 1990. *Teaching the elephant to dance: Empowering change in your organization.* New York: Crown.

Bennett, Amanda. 1991. Downsizing doesn't necessarily bring an upswing in corporate profitability. *Wall Street Journal* 6 June: B1, B4.

Bereiter, Carl, and Marlene Scardamalia. 1993. *Surpassing ourselves: An inquiry into the nature and implications of expertise.* Chicago: Open Court.

Bonner, Sarah E., Reid Hastie, Geoff B. Sprinkle, and S. Mark Young. 2000. Financial incentives and performance in laboratory tasks: Implications for management accounting. *Journal of Management Accounting Research*: 19-64.

Bond, James, Ellen Galinsky, and Jennifer Swanberg. 1998. *The 1997 national study of the changing workforce.* New York: Families and Workforce Institute.

Bower, Gordon. 1995. Emotion and cognition. In *Proceedings of the 13th Congress of Psychology, Vol. 1.*, edited by X. Gallegos and L. Hernandez. Mexico City: Trillas Co.

Boyd, E. F. 1999. Automating an order-entry process. In *Performance Interventions: Selecting, Implementing, and Evaluating the Results*, edited by Jim Fuller and Brenda Sugrue. Alexandria, VA: American Society for Training and Development.

Bransford, John, Ann L. Brown, and Rodney R. Cocking, eds. 1999. *How people learn: Brain, mind, experience, and school.* Washington, D.C.: National Academy Press.

Business Week Editors. 1994. *Business Week Guide.* New York: McGraw-Hill.

Byrne, John A. 2001. *Chainsaw: The notorious career of Al Dunlap in the era of profit-at-any-price.* New York: HarperBusiness.

Cameron, Kim S., Sarah J. Freeman, and Aneil K. Mishra. 1993. Downsizing and redesigning organizations. In *Organizational Change and Redesign*, edited by George P. Huber and William H. Glick. New York: Oxford University Press.

Chambers, Elizabeth G., Mark Foulon, Helen Handsfield-Jones, Steven M. Hankin, and Edward G. Michaels. 1998. The war for talent. *The McKinsey Quarterly* 3: 44-57.

Chi, Robert, Micheline T. H. Glaser, Robert Glaser, and Marshall J. Farr, eds. 1988. *The nature of expertise*. Hillsdale, NJ: Lawrence Erlbaum Associates.

Crichton, Michael. 1999. Ritual abuse, hot air, and missed opportunities. *Science* 284 (9 April): 238-240.

Christensen, Clayton M. 1997. *The innovator's dilemma: When new technologies cause great firms to fail*. Cambridge: Harvard Business School Press.

Christman, J. 1999. Documenting and monitoring: A performance problem solution. In *Performance interventions: Selecting, implementing, and evaluating the results*, edited by Brenda Sugrue and Jim Fuller. Alexandria, VA: American Society for Training and Development.

Clark, Richard E. 1982. Antagonism between achievement and enjoyment in ATI studies. *Educational Psychologist* 17, no. 2.

————. 1989. When teaching kills learning: Research on mathemathantics. In *Learning and instruction: European research in an international context, vol. II*, edited by H.N. Mandl, N. Bennett, E. de Corte, and H.F. Freidrich. London: Pergamon Press Ltd.

————. 1994. Media will never influence learning. *Educational Technology Research and Development* 42, no. 2: 21-29.

————. 1998. Motivating performance. *Performance Improvement* 37, no. 8: 39-47.

————. 2001. *Learning from media: Arguments, analysis and evidence*. Greenwich, CT: Information Age Publishers.

Clark, Richard E., and Fred Estes. 1996. Cognitive task analysis for training. *International Journal of Educational Research* 25, no. 5: 403-417.

————. 1998. Technology or craft: What are we doing? *Educational Technology* 38, no. 5: 5-11.

————. 1999. The development of authentic educational technologies. *Educational Technology* 39, no. 2: 5-16.

————. 2000. A proposal for the collaborative development of authentic performance technology. *Performance Improvement* 39, no. 4: 48-53.

Clark, Richard E., and Richard E. Snow. 1975. Alternative designs for instructional technology research. *AV Communication Review* 23, no. 4: 373-394.

Corkill, A., J. Glover, R. Bruning, and D. Krug. 1988. Advance organizers retrieval context hypotheses. *Journal of Educational Psychology* 80, no. 3: 304-311.

Covey, Stephen R. 1989. *The 7 habits of highly effective people*. New York: Simon & Schuster.

Cronbach, Lee J. 1966. The logic of experiments on discovery. In *Learning by discovery: A critical appraisal*, edited by L. S. Shulman and E. R. Keislar. Chicago: Rand McNally.

CSC Index. 1994. *State of reengineering report*. El Segundo, CA: Computer Sciences Corporation.

Deal, Terry E., and Allan A. Kennedy. 1999. *The new corporate cultures: Revitalizing the workplace after downsizing, mergers, and reengineering*. Reading, MA: Perseus.

Dick, Walter, Lou Carey, and James O. Carey. 2001. *The systematic design of instruction*. 5th ed. Boston: Allyn & Bacon.

Dienes, Zoltan, and Josef Perner. 1999. A theory of implicit and explicit knowledge. *Behavioral and Brain Sciences* 22, no. 5: 735-755.

Dixon, J. Robb. 1994. Business process reengineering: Improving in new strategic directions. *California Management Review* 36: 93-108.

Drucker, Peter Ferdinand. 1999. *Management challenges for the 21st century*. New York: Harper Collins.

Druckman, Daniel, Jerome E. Singer, and Harold Van Cott, eds. 1997. *Enhancing organizational performance*. Washington, D.C.: National Academy Press.

Druckman, Daniel, and Robert Bjork, eds. 1994. *Learning, remembering, and believing: Enhancing human performance*. Washington, D.C.: National Academy Press.

———. 1991. *In the mind's eye: Enhancing human performance*. Washington, D.C.: National Academy Press.

Earle, Nick, and Peter Keen. 2000. *From .com to .profit: Inventing business models that deliver value and profit*. San Francisco: Jossey Bass.

Ericsson, Anders, and Herbert Simon. 1999. *Protocol analysis: Verbal reports as data, revised edition*. Cambridge: MIT Press.

Eccles, J., and Allan Wigfield. 1995. In the mind of the actor: The structure of adolescents' achievement task values and expectancy-related beliefs. *Personality and Social Psychology Bulletin* 21: 215-225.

Estes, Fred, and Richard E. Clark. 1999. Authentic educational technology: The lynchpin between theory and practice. *Educational Technology* 39, no. 6: 5-13.

Ford, J., and D. Weissbein. 1997. Transfer of training: An updated review and analysis. *Performance Improvement Quarterly* 10, no. 2: 22-41.

Ford, Martin E. 1992. *Motivating humans: Goals, emotions and personal agency beliefs.* Newberry Park, CA: Sage.

Fuller, Jim. 1999. Achieving breakthrough sales results. In *Performance interventions: Selecting, implementing, and evaluating the results,* edited by B. Sugrue and Jim Fuller. Alexandria, VA: American Society for Training and Development.

———. 1997. *Managing performance improvement projects: Preparing, planning, implementing.* San Francisco: Jossey-Bass.

Fuller, Jim, and Jeanne Farrington. 1999. *From training to performance improvement: Navigating the transition.* San Francisco: Jossey-Bass.

Galbraith, Jay. 1995. *Designing organizations: An executive briefing on strategy, structure and processes.* San Francisco: Jossey-Bass.

Gilbert, Thomas F. 1996. *Human competence: Engineering worthy performance, tribute edition.* Washington, D.C.: International Society for Performance Improvement.

Gilovich, Thomas. 1991. *How we know what isn't so: The fallibility of human reason in everyday life.* New York: Free Press.

Glaser, Robert. 1990. The re emergence of learning theory within instructional research. *American Psychologist* 45, no. 1: 29-39.

Glaser, Robert, Allan Lesgold, S. Lajoie, R. Eastman, L. Greenberg, D. Logan, Maria Magone, A. Weiner, R. Wolf, and L. Yengo. 1985. *Cognitive task analysis to enhance technical skills training and assessment.* (Final Report to the Air Force Human Resources Laboratory on Contract No. F41689-8v3-C-0029.) Pittsburgh: Learning Research and Development Center, University of Pittsburgh.

Glaser, Robert, Allan Lesgold, and Sherrie Gott. 1991. Implications of cognitive psychology for measuring job performance. In *Performance assessment for the workplace, volume II: Technical issues,* edited by Alexandra K. Wigdor and Bert F. Green, Jr. National Research Council. Washington, DC: National Academy Press.

Golembiewski, Robert T., and Ben-Chu Sun. 1990. Positive-finding bias in QWL studies: Rigor and outcomes in a large sample. *Journal of Management* 16: 665-674.

Goldberg, L. R. 1993. The structure of phenotypic personality traits. *American Psychologist* 48, no. 1: 26-34.

Gordon, Jack, and Ron Zemke. 2000. The attack on ISD. *Training* 37, no. 4 (April): 42.

Greenbaum, Thomas L. 1998. *The handbook for focus group research*. Beverly Hills: Sage.

Hamel, Gary, and Coimbatore K. Prahalad. 1994. *Competing for the future*. Cambridge: Harvard Business School Press.

Hardt, Jonathan, and Judith Rodin. 1999. Control and efficacy as interdisciplinary bridges. *Review of General Psychology* 3, no. 4: 317-337.

Henkoff, R. 1990. Cost cutting: How to do it right. *Fortune* (9 April): 17-19.

Hill, J. 2000. Executive overconfidence. Ph.D. diss., Rossier School of Education, University of Southern California, Los Angeles.

Hoffrage, U., R. Hertwig, and G. Gigerenzer. 2000. Hindsight bias. *Journal of Experimental Psychology: Learning, memory and cognition* 26, no. 3.

Karau, Steven J., and Kip D. Williams. 1993. Social loafing: A meta-analytic review and theoretical integration. *Journal of Personality and Social Psychology* 65, no. 4: 681-706.

———. 1995. Social loafing: Research findings, implications, and future directions. *Current Directions* 4: 134-139.

Katz, J. 1997. The wired citizen. *Wired* 82 (December).

Kaufman, Roger A. 1996. *Strategic thinking: A guide to identifying and solving problems*. Alexandria, VA: American Society for Training and Development and International Society for Performance Improvement.

———. 2000. MegaPlanning: Practical tools for organizational success. Newberry Park, CA: Sage.

Kirkpatrick, Donald L. 1998. *Evaluating training programs: The four levels*. San Francisco: Barrett-Koehler Publishers.

Kirsch, Irving, and Steven Jay Lynn. 1999. Automaticity in clinical psychology. *American Psychologist* 54, no. 7: 504-515.

Klein, R. 1999. Commitment. *Journal of Applied Psychology* 84, no. 6: 885-896.

Kluger, Avraham, and Angelo DiNisi. 1998. Feedback interventions: Toward the understanding of a double-edged sword. *Current Directions in Psychological Science* 7, no. 3: 67-72.

Levin, Henry M., and Patrick J. McEwan. 2000. *Cost effectiveness analysis: Methods and applications*. 2d ed. Beverly Hills: SAGE Publications.

Locke, Edwin A., and Gary P. Latham. 1990. *A theory of goal setting and task performance*. Englewood Cliffs, NJ: Prentice-Hall.

McDonald, D., and A. Smith. 1995. A proven connection: Performance management and business results. *Compensation and Benefits Review* (January-February).

McKinley, William. 1992. Decreasing organizational size: To untangle or not to untangle? *Academy of Management Review* 17: 112-123.

Mager, Robert F. 1997. *Making instruction work or skillbloomers: A step-by-step guide to designing and developing instruction that works*. 2d ed. Atlanta: The Center for Effective Performance, Inc.

———. 1997. *Goal analysis: how to clarify your goals so you can actually achieve them*. 3d ed. Atlanta: The Center for Effective Performance, Inc.

Maharaj, Davan. 1998. End of the "Chainsaw Al" era? *Los Angeles Times*, 16 June.

Martin, James. 1991. *Rapid application development*. New York: Macmillan.

Merrill, M. David. 2001. First principles of instruction. http://www.id2.usu.edu/Papers/5FirstPrinciples.PDF

Morrisey, George L. 1996. *A guide to long-range planning: Creating your strategic journey*. San Francisco: Jossey-Bass.

Morrow, Charley, M. Quintin Jarrett, and Melvin Rupinsky. 1997. An investigation of the effect and economic utility of corporate-wide training. *Personnel Psychology* 50: 91-119.

National Center on the Educational Quality of the Workforce (EQW). 1995. *The other shoe: Education's contribution to the productivity of establishments*. Catalog No. RE02.

National Research Council (NRC). 1996. *National science education standards*. Washington, D.C.: National Academy Press.

Newman, G. A., J. E. Edwards, and N. S. Raju. 1989. Organizational development interventions: A meta-analysis of their effects on satisfaction and other attitudes. *Personnel Psychology* 42: 461-489.

Norman, Donald A. 1988. *The psychology of everyday things*. New York: Basic Books.

O'Neal, Charles, and Kate Bertrand. 1991. *Developing a winning JIT marketing strategy*. Englewood Cliffs, NJ: Prentice Hall.

Packard, David. 1995. *The HP way: How Bill Hewlett and I built our company*. New York: HarperCollins.

Parker, Louise E. 1993. When to fix it and when to leave: Relationships among perceived control, self-efficacy, dissent, and exit. *Journal of Applied Psychology* 78: 949-959.

Pelham, B., and E. Neter. 1995. The effect of motivational judgment depends on the difficulty of the judgment. *Journal of Personality and Social Psychology* 68, no. 4: 581-594.

Pendergast, Canice. 1999. The provision of incentives in firms. *Journal of Economic Literature* 37: 7-63.

Pervin, Lawrence, and Oliver John, eds. 1999. *Handbook of personality: Theory and research*. New York: Gilford.

Peters, Thomas J., and Robert H. Waterman. 1982. *In search of excellence: Lessons from America's best-run companies*. New York: Warner Brothers.

Phillips, Jack J. 1991. *Handbook of training evaluation and measurement methods*. 3d ed. Houston: Gulf Publishing.

———. 1994. *Measuring return on investment*. Alexandria, VA: American Society for Training and Development.

———. 1997. *Return on investment in training and performance improvement programs*. Houston: Gulf Publishing.

Pintrich, Paul, and Dale Schunk. 1996. *Motivation in education: Theory, research and applications*. Englewood Cliffs, NJ: Merrill.

Pittenger, David J. 1993a. Measuring the MBTI...and coming up short. *Journal of Career Planning and Employment* 54: 48-53.

———. 1993b. The utility of the Myers-Briggs Type Indicator. *Review of Educational Research* 63: 467-488.

Porter, Michael E. 1998. *Competitive advantage: Creating and sustaining superior performance*. New York: Free Press.

———. 1980. *Competitive strategy: Techniques for analyzing industries and competitors*. New York: Free Press.

Reel, S. 1999. Preventing ergonomic injury while reducing cycle time. In *Performance Interventions: Selecting, Implementing, and Evaluating the Results*, edited by Brenda Sugrue and Jim Fuller. Alexandria, VA: American Society for Training and Development.

Resnick, Lauren B. 1987. *Education and learning to think*. Washington, D.C.: National Academy Press.

Rossett, Allison. 1999. *First things fast: A handbook for performance analysis*. San Francisco: Jossey-Bass Pfeiffer.

———. 1987. *Training needs assessment*. Englewood Cliffs, NJ: Educational Technology Publications.

Rother, Mike, and John Shook. 1998. *Learning to see: Value stream mapping to create value and Eliminate Muda*, v.1.1.Brookline MA: The Lean Enterprise Institute.

Rummler, Geary, and Alan Brache. 1995. *Improving performance: Managing the white space in organizations*. 2d ed. San Francisco: Jossey-Bass.

Salomon, Garriel. 1983. The differential investment of effort in learning from different sources. *Educational Psychologist*: 18, no. 1: 42-50.

———. 1984. Television is "easy" and print is "tough": The differential investment of mental effort in learning as a function of perceptions and attributions. *Journal of Educational Psychology* 76: 774-786.

Schraagen, Jan Maarten, Susan F. Chipman, and Valerie L. Shalin. 2000. *Cognitive task analysis*. Mahwah, NJ: Lawrence Erlbaum Associates.

Schwartz, Peter. 1991. *The art of the long view: Planning for the future in an uncertain world*. New York: Doubleday.

Schweiger, David M., and Angelo S. DeNisi. 1991. Communication with employees following a merger: A longitudinal field experiment. *Academy of Management Journal* 34: 110-135.

Science. 1999. 284 (9 April): 238-240.

Senge, Peter. 1990. *The fifth discipline: The art and practice of the learning organization*. New York: Doubleday.

Shadid, W. 1993. Intercultural communication in the medical care sector. In *Culture, development and communication*, edited by W. Shadid and P. J. M. Nas. Leiden: CNWS.

Spitzer, Dean. 1995. *SuperMotivation*. New York: AMACOM Books.

Stolovitch, Harold 1997. Introduction to the Special Issue on Transfer of Training-Transfer of Learning. *Performance Improvement Quarterly* 10, no. 2: 5-6.

Stolovitch, Harold, and Erica Keeps, eds. 1999. *Handbook of Human Performance Technology: Improving individual and organizational performance worldwide*. 2d ed. San Francisco: Jossey-Bass.

Sugrue, Brenda, and Jim Fuller, eds. 1999. *Performance interventions: Selecting, implementing, and evaluating the results*. Washington, D.C.: American Society for Training and Development.

Sweller, J. 1994. Cognitive load theory, learning difficulty, and instructional design. *Learning and Instruction* 4: 295-312.

Swoboda, F. 1995. Corporate downsizing goes global. *Washington Post News Service. Ann Arbor News* (April 11): A8.

Thiagarajan, Sivasailam, Fred Estes, and Frances Kemmerer. 1999. Designing compensation systems to motivate performance improvement. In *The Handbook of Human Performance Technology*, edited by Harold Stolevitch and E. Keeps. San Francisco: Jossey-Bass Pfeiffer.

Tobias, Sigmund, and J. D. Fletcher, eds. 2000. *Training and retraining: A handbook for business, industry, government and the military*. New York: Macmillan Reference.

Training. 1992. Industry report. (October): 43.

Van Merrienboer, Jeroen J. G. 1997. *Training complex cognitive skills: A four-component instructional design model for technical training*. Englewood Cliffs, NJ: Educational Technology Publications.

Van Merrienboer, Jeroen J.G., Richard E. Clark, and M. B. M. de Croock. In press. The 4/CID*-model part 1: Blueprints for complex learning. *Educational Technology Research and Development*.

Williams, Kip D., and Steven J. Karau. 1991. Social loafing and social compensation: The effects of expectations of coworker performance. *Journal of Personality and Social Psychology* 61: 570-581.

Winter, D. 1996. Ecological psychology: Healing the spirit between planet and self. New York: HarperCollins.

Index

About the Authors

RICHARD E. CLARK is currently a professor of Educational Psychology and Technology in the Rossier School of Education at the University of Southern California, where he directs a doctoral program in Human Performance at Work. He was chosen as the 2002 recipient of the prestigious Thomas F. Gilbert Professional Achievement Award by the International Society for Performance Improvement. He has served as a performance improvement specialist in a great variety of organizations in North and South America, Europe, Africa, and Asia in the past two decades. For two years he served as Program Board Member and lecturer in Organizational Psychology at Dublin City University in Ireland, and he is Professeur Associé at the Université de Montréal, Faculté des sciences de l' éducation in Montréal, Québec. He was also a senior lecturer at the IKIP Jakarta, Indonesia during the 1980s. He was selected as a Fulbright lecturer in Spain and has been a visiting professor in South Africa (University of Witwatersrand), the Netherlands (University of Twente), and a Ford Foundation Scholar in Residence at the Ministry of Education in Bogota, Columbia. He is president of Atlantic Training Inc., a consulting company with offices in Los Angeles and Dublin. Clark's interest is in the performance of people and technology in culturally diverse, multinational organizations where complex knowledge work is accomplished in a constantly changing environment. He is the author of more than 150 published books, chapters, articles, and monographs, including, most recently, *Learning from Media: Arguments, Analysis, and Evidence* (Information Age Publishing Inc., 2001), which sold out its first print run in advance of the book's release. He is an Educational Psychologist who is an elected Fellow in the American Psychological Association, the American Psychological Society and the American Association of Applied Psychology.

FRED ESTES has worked for many years managing training design and performance improvement projects for large companies, including Hewlett-Packard and Bank of America, as well as small, high-technology startups. Estes has worked as an internal performance consultant, an instructional designer, and an education program manager. His doctorate is in Educational Psychology and Technology and he serves as an adjunct professor at the University of Southern California and San Jose State University. In addition, he teaches at the Nueva School and manages Knowledge/ Design, a performance consultancy. Estes has published in professional journals in the areas of performance consulting, learning, authentic technology, and cognitive task analysis, as well as contributing chapters to the *Handbook of Human Performance Technology* and other edited books.

The authors chose to work together on this book partly because they represent two complementary points of view and experience in different settings and contexts. As a team, the authors balance their advice by weighing their separate insights about performance that derive from each of their two different "work cultures."

Made in the USA
Las Vegas, NV
28 March 2022

46371178R00122